The
NATURAL HISTORY
of
NEW JERSEY

Written by Stan Freeman
Illustrated by Mike Nasuti

New Jersey Statehouse in Trenton

Red fox

Daisy fleabane

Canada goose

Bumblebee

Hampshire House Publishing Co.

Florence, Mass.

Eastern screech owl chicks

CONTENTS

American toad

Great blue heron

Garter snake

Eastern chipmunk

Red-tailed hawk

Raccoon

Water lily

NEW JERSEY

Fast facts

Capital: Trenton

Population (2015 est.): 8,958,013, 11th among all states

Population density: 1210/square mile, 1st among all states

Total area: 8,722 square miles, 47th among all states

Geographic center: In Mercer County, 5 miles southeast of Trenton

Counties

1 - Sussex
2 - Passaic
3 - Bergen
4 - Warren
5 - Morris
6 - Essex
7 - Hudson
8 - Union
9 - Hunterdon
10 - Somerset

11 - Middlesex
12 - Mercer
13 - Monmouth
14 - Ocean
15 - Burlington
16 - Camden
17 - Gloucester
18 - Atlantic
19 - Salem
20 - Cumberland
21 - Cape May

Dimensions

59 miles
37 miles
168 miles

New Jersey's population

Year	Population	Year	Population
1800	211,149	1920	3,155,900
1820	277,575	1940	4,160,165
1840	373,306	1960	6,066,782
1860	672,035	1980	7,365,011
1880	1,131,116	2000	8,414,891
1900	1,883,669	2015 (est.)	8,958,013

New Jersey's largest municipalities (as of 2014)

City	Population
Newark	280,579
Jersey City	262,146
Paterson	146,753
Elizabeth	128,705
Edison	101,970
Woodbridge	100,824

The Statue of Liberty in New York Harbor, with Jersey City on the left shore and Manhattan on the right shore

A little more than a century ago, America was not a land where the deer and the antelope played or the buffalo roamed. Populations of these animals and others had been reduced to the point that the survival of some species was very much in doubt.

Similarly, parts of the Northeast were nearly barren of many species of wildlife that had lived here for thousands of years, including black bears, moose and beavers.

The cutting of forests, plowing of meadows, damming of rivers and unrestricted hunting had taken their toll on wildlife.

To halt the decline in animal populations, laws that regulated hunting were established in many states in the early 1900s. This worked well for some animals, such as black bears and white-tailed deer, which gradually returned on their own to areas they had once inhabited.

In the case of animals that did not return on their own, wildlife biologists tried to raise them on game farms for release into the wild, or they captured wild animals in other states for release locally.

However, it was not enough to return these once-native animals to their historic territories. Their habitats – the land and water – also had to be restored. Loss of habitat is the primary reason most species of plants and animals

The bald eagle, once the symbol of vanishing wildlife, is no longer endangered nationally although breeding eagles are still endangered in New Jersey.

become rare or endangered. So thousands of acres of forests were bought to establish state and federal forests, parks and wildlife refuges, and rivers that had been fouled with sewage and trash were gradually cleaned.

If animals were to be restored, they also had to be protected. In 1973, the federal Endangered Species Act was passed, making it a crime to hunt or otherwise harm many species of rare plants and animals. In addition, laws were passed in each state to protect plants or animals that were rare or endangered in that state.

State laws were also passed to protect wetland areas and water bodies, such as ponds, lakes, marshes and rivers. All living things depend on water for survival, and areas where land and water come together, such as the land surrounding a stream or river, are among the richest habitats for plants and animals. Red-winged blackbirds and marsh wrens nest in the cattails of pond edges. Beavers build their lodges in ponds and marshes. Muskrats and river otters live much of their lives in water.

Today in New Jersey, there are perhaps 3,000 species of plants and animals considered native to the state. That does not even include the unknown number of invertebrate species – mainly insects.

New Jersey's rare native species

Governments have set up a system to classify the health of populations of plants and animals. A species is considered endangered if it is on the verge of extinction in its natural range. It is threatened if it is likely to become endangered in the near future. It is on the federal endangered species list if it is endangered or threatened nationwide. It is on the state list if it is endangered or threatened in New Jersey even though it may be more common in other states.

Protected New Jersey species as of 2015

	Endangered state list/ federal list	Threatened state list/ federal list
Mammals	9/8	0/0
Birds[1]	20/1	14/1
Reptiles	8/3	3/3
Amphibians	3/0	3/0
Fish[2]	2/2	0/0
Invertebrates[3]	10/3	14/1
Plants	356/1	0/5
Total	408/18	34/10

[1] The breeding populations of bald eagles and black rails are endangered but the non-breeding populations are threatened
[2] Includes inland freshwater fish only
[3] Includes butterflies, moths, beetles, dragonflies, crustaceans, mussels, snails, worms and sponges

Federal endangered species list includes these New Jersey natives:
Humpback whale
Roseate tern
Leatherback seaturtle
Dwarf wedgemussel
Chaffseed
Indiana bat
Mitchell's satyr

State endangered species list includes:
All N.J. species on the federal list
Peregrine falcon
Arogos skipper
Blue-spotted salamander
Short-eared owl
Queen snake
Saltmarsh bulrush

Great spangled fritillary, a native species

Black-eyed Susan, a native species

Invaders

Just like many Americans, many plants can trace their roots to foreign soils. There are also animals found in New Jersey that have ties to other places in America or abroad.

A range of wildflowers, trees, insects, fish, birds and other life forms were brought to the region over the years by gardeners, naturalists, cooks and sportsmen who admired them elsewhere and released them – or allowed them to escape – into the wild here.

Others came as accidental hitchhikers on trucks, cars and airplanes and as stowaways on early sailing ships and ocean freighters. Still others arrived here on their own as part of the natural spread of their species into places where they could survive.

While the vast majority don't harm local ecosystems, a small percentage do. Called "invasives," these aggressive species invade and dominate the landscapes on which they alight, pushing out valued native species. Some naturalists estimate that only about two-thirds of the plants found in the state were here before Europeans arrived. However, only two or three dozen of these late arrivals are considered seriously invasive.

For instance, purple loosestrife was introduced from Europe as a garden flower and eventually escaped into the wild. It has strikingly beautiful flowers, but it can quickly take over a wetland, such as a marsh, pushing out native

Oriental bittersweet, an invasive species introduced from Asia

plant species, some of them important to nesting wetland birds.

European starlings, which were also natives of Europe, were released in Central Park in New York City in the early 1890's by Shakespeare fans who wanted to introduce to America the birds mentioned in the immortal writer's plays.

They have since spread from coast to coast and are reducing the populations of some other birds. Starlings nest in tree cavities, taking away nesting sites from other cavity-nesters such as bluebirds, northern flickers and tree swallows.

Oriental bittersweet, introduced from Asia, is a fast-growing vine common to back yards that wraps around shrubs, trees and flowers, forming a thick tangle in which native species perish. In the fall it produces reddish-orange berries.

At least one species of harmful invader, the gypsy moth, was the result of a breeding experiment gone wrong. In 1869, hoping to start a silk business, a Massachusetts man tried to cross imported European gypsy moths with silk moths to create a more productive silkworm. The breeding attempt failed, but some of the moth larvae accidentally escaped. Gypsy moths have now spread through most of the East.

In most years, the gypsy moth caterpillars, which feed on tree leaves, defoliate more than a million acres of forests.

Purple loosestrife, an invasive species introduced from Europe

European starling, an invasive species introduced from Europe

Barn owl

From northern cardinals and black-capped chickadees to great horned owls and bald eagles, the skies can seem nearly as populated with birds as the land is with people.

In fact, more populated. It's estimated there may be 20 times as many birds on Earth as humans. Walk through any field or forest in summer and you can easily believe it.

Nearly 370 species of birds can be seen at least once a year in New Jersey, including about 210 that nest in the state. In all of North America, more than 800 species of birds have been reported. Worldwide, there may be more than 10,000 species of birds.

While large forests in the state attract their share of birds that seek isolation from humans, such as scarlet tanagers and hermit thrushes, cities and suburbs are home to birds that can easily live around people, such as American goldfinches and mourning doves.

Nearly 150 million years ago, the first birds were appearing on Earth. But they may have looked more like winged lizards than modern birds. Birds, like most creatures, have changed, or evolved, over millions of years to have specialized features that help them survive by giving them an advantage over other living things. For most birds, the most important feature is the ability to fly and to live much of their lives above ground and in the air.

Even among birds, though, different species have

Cedar waxwing

evolved to have different features – variations in size, coloring, wing design or body shape. Because of these physical differences, some birds can find food in ways that others can't, or they can live and nest in places where others can't. As a result, more kinds of birds can survive than would be possible if all birds ate the same foods and lived and nested in the same places.

Birds born with a difference that gives them an advantage in finding food, such as a slightly longer beak, or an advantage in escaping predators, such as greater flying speed, are more likely to survive and have young. Therefore, their special features are more likely to be passed along to future generations.

Using this process, called natural selection, woodpeckers developed over millions of years to have strong, sharp beaks, long tongues and sharp claws. They use their claws to grab onto the sides of trees, and they use their beaks to peck nest holes in trees and to dig beneath bark to find insects. They use their long tongues to grab the insects they find.

Herons and egrets developed to have long, thin legs and long, sharp beaks. They use their legs to wade in the shallow water of lakes, streams and ponds. They can stand very still and wait for fish or tadpoles to pass by so that they can spear them with their beaks. To a fish, their thin legs may look like reeds.

Artists of the air

Birds do not merely fly. They also hover, soar and glide. If there are artists of the air, though, it may be the hummingbirds. They have made an art of functional flight.

Hummingbirds evolved to have strong wing muscles for a specific purpose. They can beat their wings very rapidly, on average 55 times each second, to hover at flowers like bumblebees, so that they can use their long beaks and tongues to sip the energy-rich nectar inside flowers.

A female ruby-throated hummingbird

A male ruby-throated hummingbird

In the Northeast, songbirds (a category that includes most backyard birds) usually nest and lay their eggs from April to June. For smaller birds, like the tufted titmouse, white-breasted nuthatch and tree swallow, the eggs take about two weeks to hatch, and the young stay in the nest two to three weeks before they take their first flights.

For larger birds, such as great horned owls and red-tailed hawks, the eggs may take nearly four weeks to hatch, and the young may remain in the nest four to six weeks.

Birds in the wild have varying life spans. Harsh weather, accidents, predators, disease and lack of food can take their toll. Most songbirds live only two to five years.

American robin

However, some larger birds, such as mallards and great blue herons, may live 20 years or more.

Birds are often specialists about food. Many species prefer one type of food. Canada geese like grass, eagles prefer fish, finches look for seeds and warblers like insects. However, most birds will eat more than one kind of food, and some will change their diet as the seasons change.

Generally, the larger a bird is, the faster it can fly. Finches and sparrows can reach top flying speeds of about 20 miles per hour, hawks can fly 30 to 40 miles per hour and geese, when pressed, can fly 60 miles per hour. Peregrine falcons, which hunt from the air, may be capable of the fastest flying speeds,

Backyard birds of New Jersey

Some birds will nest in residential areas. Shown for the birds below is: Nest construction – Average number of eggs per brood – Broods per season – Period during which eggs are laid – Time to hatching – Time to nestlings' first flights

Blue jay
A cup of rootlets, twigs, bark strips and leaves, usually in an evergreen tree 10 to 25 feet off the ground – Four or five eggs – One brood – Early April to early July – About 17 days – About 19 days

Ruby-throated hummingbird
A small cup of plant down, fibers and spider silk built in the fork of a drooping limb, usually 10 to 20 feet off the ground – Two eggs – One or two broods – Mid-May to mid-July – About 16 days – About 19 days

Black-capped chickadee
A cavity in a standing dead tree lined with cottony fibers, fur, moss, hair, wool and feathers, usually 4 to 10 feet off the ground – Six to eight eggs – One brood – Mid-April to mid-July – About 12 days – About 16 days

American robin
A deep cup made of grasses and weed stalks and shaped with mud in the fork of a tree branch, in shrubs or on a window ledge, usually 5 to 15 feet off the ground – Three or four eggs – Two, rarely three broods – Mid-March to mid-July – About 12 days – About 15 days

Downy woodpecker
A cavity in a living or dead tree, usually 20 to 30 feet off the ground – Four or five eggs – One brood – Early May to late June – About 12 days – About 21 days

Northern cardinal
A shallow cup of twigs, grasses, rootlets and vines in dense shrubs or thickets or in an evergreen tree, usually less than 10 feet off the ground – Three or four eggs – Two or three broods – Early April to early August – About 12 days – About 12 days

House sparrow
A cavity lined with grasses, weeds and feathers in a tree, on a building, on a billboard or in a birdhouse, usually 10 to 50 feet off the ground – Four to six eggs – Two or three broods – Early April to early August – About 12 days – About 16 days

Blue jay

Northern cardinal

up to 200 miles per hour. They dive rapidly on their prey, usually other birds in flight, killing them with the impact of the collision.

Feathers are a bird's clothing, keeping it warm in winter and giving it a colorful appearance. A robin may have 3,000 feathers. A tundra swan may have 25,000. However, most birds replace their feathers once or twice a year, a process called molting. The molt may take a month or more to complete.

Some birds, such as male American goldfinches, grow their brightest feathers for the breeding season, when they are trying to attract mates. Then they grow duller-colored feathers for the winter, which makes them less visible to predators.

Since it is most often the male's job to attract a female, in many species, including northern cardinals and American goldfinches, the male has brighter feather coloring than the female. With her plain coloring that often blends in with surrounding vegetation, the female does not draw as much attention to the nest and young.

Eggs
Some bird eggs shown their actual size

For many birds, the color and markings on their eggs have a purpose – to act as camouflage. For birds that build cup nests off the ground, such as cedar waxwings, the base color of their eggs is usually cream or buff and the markings may be streaks or speckles of brown. For birds, such as terns and gulls, that build nests on the ground, where predators are even more of a threat, the camouflage of streaks and speckles can be even more of a necessity. For birds that lay their eggs in darkened holes in trees, such as some owls, the color usually does not matter.

Canada goose

American crow

Great horned owl

Cedar waxwing

American robin

Yellow warbler

Ruby-throated hummingbird

A robin's nest

When a robin's nest shows up unexpectedly on a family's window sill in spring, it instantly becomes a made-to-order field experiment and one of the most compelling entries into the natural sciences that young kids will encounter.

Robins love the worms found in residential lawns, and they are not shy about building their nests near or on a home – or even on a back-yard deck, as in this pictured nest.

In New Jersey, robins lay their eggs from mid-March to mid-July in cup-shaped nests made of grasses and weed stalks plastered together with mud. The nests might be built in the fork of tree branches or on a protected flat surface of a home.

With their distinctive sky-blue coloring, the eggs hatch in about 12 days. The fragile hatchlings initially weigh about a fifth of an ounce. As a comparison, that's about the weight of two pennies. But within two weeks, when they are ready to take their first flights, they will weigh nearly 2.5 ounces – about the weight of 12 quarters and about the size of an adult robin. And that means they will have to eat a lot in a short time to gain weight so rapidly.

Robin eggs in a nest

Females do most of the incubation of the eggs, as is the case for most songbirds. But when it comes to feeding the young, both parents do their part.

In the first few days, the parents feed the young swallowed food that they bring back to their mouths, but about day three or four, the nestlings begin eating whole foods, mainly worms and insects.

Studies have found the parents bring food to the nest six to seven times an hour, on average, so that each nestling gets 35 to 40 feedings per day. The parents bring about 200 grams of food to the nest each day, or about seven ounces. That amounts to more than six pounds of wriggly crawly things fed to the young before they leave the nest.

When young robins finally take their first flight about two weeks after hatching, it is usually an awkward trip from the nest to the ground, as they are not yet capable of full flight. The parents may lead them to the protection of shrubs or undergrowth, and they will continue to feed them for several days until they develop the skills to survive on their own.

One day old

Three days old

Two weeks old

Food for the young

A feeding

Barn swallows build nests of mud and straw that are plastered to building structures.

The stick nests of bald eagles are built high in trees and are used year after year.

Killdeer nests are built on the ground in open areas.

Hummingbird nests are often held together with spider silk.

Nests

Different species of birds build different kinds of nests. One of the most common types is a cup-shaped nest built with grass or twigs in the fork created by two branches of a tree. However, birds also build nests on the ground, atop buildings, on billboards, in barns, on mountain ledges and in holes in trees.

House wrens have been known to build a nest in a discarded shoe, a tin can, a teapot or in the pocket of a shirt hanging on a clothesline.

The largest nests are those of eagles. Some are eight feet across, 15 feet deep, and weigh as much as a small automobile.

The smallest nests are those of hummingbirds. Some are less than an inch across and the eggs are the size of peas.

Pileated woodpeckers peck holes in trees for their nests.

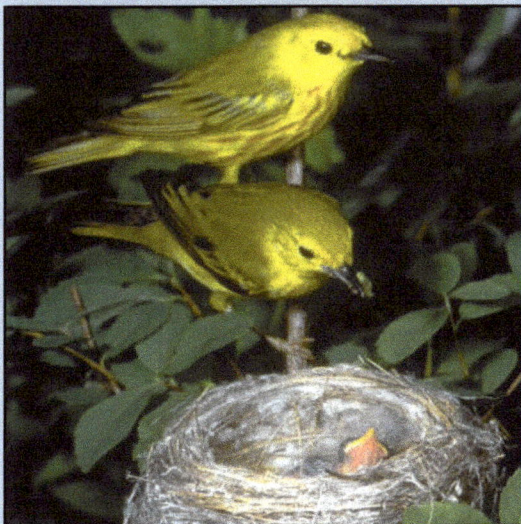

Yellow warblers build nests of milkweed fibers, plant down, hemp and grasses.

The common loon builds its nest by the water using grass, reeds, twigs and rushes. (It visits but generally does not nest in the state.)

Cedar waxwings at their nest

An eastern bluebird entering its nest in a tree hole

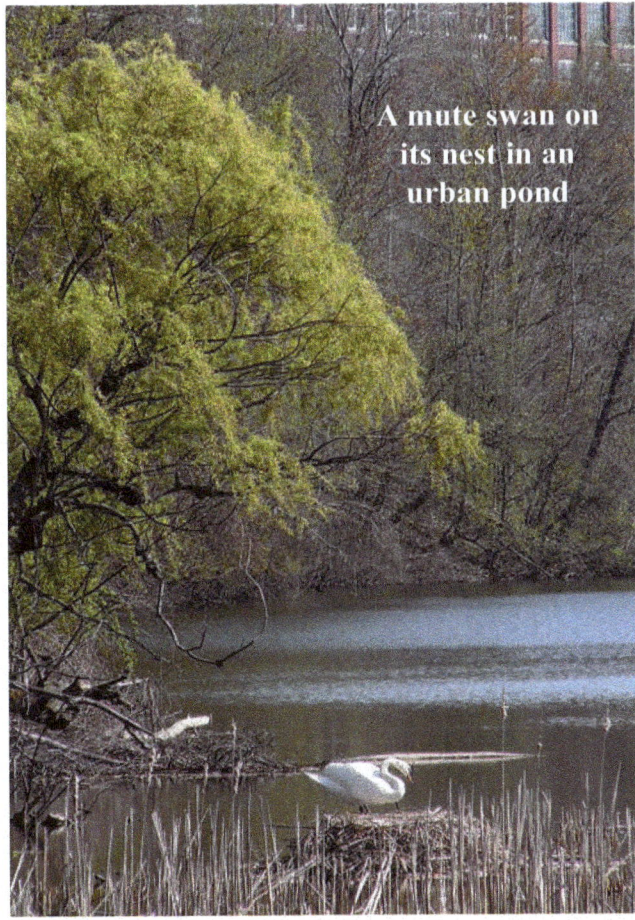

A mute swan on its nest in an urban pond

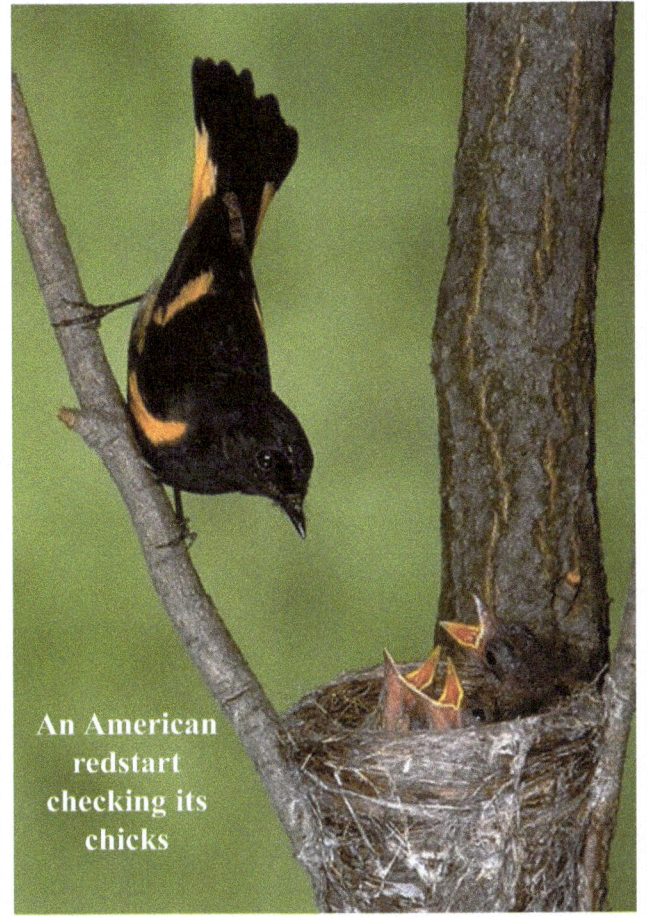

An American redstart checking its chicks

A northern cardinal feeding its young

American goldfinch

Tufted titmouse

Mourning dove

Great horned owl

Baltimore oriole

Songs and calls

The songs and calls of birds are their language. They use these sounds to tell other birds a territory is theirs, to attract a mate and to warn of danger, among other things. Their songs and calls may sound like this:

TUFTED TITMOUSE – "Peter! Peter! Peter!"
MOURNING DOVE – "Coo-ah, coo, coo, coo!"
GRAY CATBIRD – "Meow!"
OVENBIRD – "Teacher, teacher, teacher!"
GREAT HORNED OWL – "Who, who-who-who, who, who!"
EASTERN TOWHEE – "Drink your tea!"
BALTIMORE ORIOLE – "Hew-lee!"
WHITE-THROATED SPARROW – "Poor Sam Peabody, Peabody, Peabody!"
AMERICAN GOLDFINCH – "Potato chip!"
RED-WINGED BLACKBIRD – "Ok-a-lee!"
COMMON YELLOWTHROAT – "Witchity, witchity, witchity, witch!"
BLUE JAY – "Thief! Thief!" or "Jay! Jay!"

Migration

Because northern winters can be harsh and food can be scarce, many birds migrate in the fall to warmer regions in the southern United States and Central and South America. Then they return in the spring. However, some birds stay in New Jersey through the winter, including northern cardinals, blue jays and crows. Some birds of a species, like the eastern bluebird, will stay in the state through the winter, but most migrate south.

During the migration, birds may travel 200 to 300 miles a day. Some, like hawks and ducks, travel during daylight hours, but most smaller birds travel at night when they are less visible to predators.

Range and migration routes for the scarlet tanager

- Range during the breeding season
- Migration routes
- Range during winter

Typical migration times in New Jersey

	Arrival	Departure
Eastern bluebird	Early March	Oct.
Song sparrow	Late March, early April	Sept., Oct.
Eastern meadowlark	Mid-March, early April	Oct.
House wren	Late April, early May	Sept.
Broad-winged hawk	Late April	Mid-Sept.
Yellow warbler	Early May	Late July, early Aug.
Barn swallow	Late April, early May	Mid-Aug.
Baltimore oriole	Early May	Late Aug., early Sept.
Scarlet tanager	Mid-May	Sept.

CHECKLIST
Common birds

Red-winged blackbird
8 in. from tip of beak to tip of tail
☐

Eastern bluebird
6 in.
☐

Northern cardinal
8 in.
M   F
☐

Black-capped chickadee
5 in.
☐

American crow
19 in.
☐

Mourning dove
12 in.

Rock dove (pigeon)
13 in.

House finch
6 in.

Northern flicker
13 in.

American goldfinch
5 in.
M
F

Canada goose
38 in.

Common grackle
12 in.

Ring-billed gull
19 in.

Great blue heron
48 in.

Ruby-throated hummingbird
3 in.
M
F

Blue jay
12 in.

Dark-eyed junco
6 in.

Belted kingfisher
13 in.

Mallard
23 in.

Northern mockingbird
11 in.

White-breasted nuthatch
6 in.

Baltimore oriole
8 in.

American robin
10 in.

House sparrow
6 in.

Song sparrow
6 in.

White-throated sparrow
7 in.

European starling
8 in.

Tree swallow
6 in.

Tufted titmouse
6 in.

Cedar waxwing
7 in.

Downy woodpecker
6 in.

House wren
5 in.

Woodpeckers

How do these tree-pounding birds avoid headaches?

It's like banging your head against a brick wall – in fact, too much like it.

Woodpeckers have certainly earned their name. They peck on trees to create nesting holes, to find insects beneath the bark and to communicate with other woodpeckers. But the loud, rapid rat-a-tat-tat of of a woodpecker is produced with such force that it would likely cause death or severe brain damage in any other living thing that tried it.

Indeed, the force with which these head-banging birds strike a tree is at least 13 times more than the force of a car crash that would kill or severely injure the average man, woman or child, studies have found. Yet, they can peck 20 times a second and more than 12,000 times a day without apparent damage.

How do they survive the tremendous blows to their head? It's because their skulls and bodies have evolved to have features that cushion the impact and protect the brain.

It's estimated that 99.7 percent of the force of the striking blow of the beak is absorbed by the body, not the brain. And the energy that is absorbed by the brain is mainly turned to heat. That's one reason why a woodpecker tends to peck in short bursts. When it stops, the brain's temperature has a chance to return closer to normal.

When a woodpecker is pecking, it moves around the posi-

Northern flicker

tion of its head to prevent any one spot of their brain from getting too much of a pounding. And in critical places, the bones of the skull have a "spongy" structure, which allows them to absorb much of the energy of the peck before it reaches the brain. Also, unlike humans, whose brains are loosely packed in their skulls, a woodpecker's brain is tightly packed so that there is little space between the brain and skull, which means the brain does not rattle around during a peck's impact.

One feature of a woodpecker's skull is especially helpful. There is a bone, called the hyoid bone, that wraps around its brain, acting like a seat belt to hold it in place during pecking. And its design diverts much of the energy of the pecking away from the brain.

As for the beak of a woodpecker, it is very sharp and the pecking drives it into the wood rather than bluntly hammering it. Also, the upper beak is slightly longer than the lower beak, which means the upper beak absorbs more of the force of a peck. That energy travels along the upper beak to where it encounters the hyoid bone, which sends the force away from the brain.

Two other features also help woodpeckers survive their hammering. Thick neck muscles absorb much of the energy of the pecking, and a third inner eyelid closes on impact, preventing the bird's eyeballs from popping out of its head as it noisily pounds away on a tree.

Common woodpeckers

Hairy woodpecker

Downy woodpecker
6 inches, tip of the beak to end of the tail

Yellow-bellied sapsucker
8 inches

Hairy woodpecker
10 inches
(Looks very much like the downy but has a proportionately longer bill)

Red-bellied woodpecker
11 inches

Northern flicker
12 inches
(Often seen hunting ants on the ground)

Pileated woodpecker
18 inches

Yellow-bellied sapsucker

Red-bellied woodpecker

Pileated woodpecker

Downy woodpecker

Raptors

Raptors are the rulers of the skies. Eagles, hawks, falcons, owls and other birds of prey (as raptors are also called) have features that are standards of excellence in the animal world. Consider the sharp eyes of an eagle, the keen hearing of an owl or the breathtaking speed of a diving falcon. Throughout the Northeast, the populations of many species of these raptors are soaring. It has become common now to see a red-tailed hawk sitting high on a roadside tree or an American kestrel perched on a telephone wire.

In the 1960s, though, some species of raptors were headed for extinction. A widely used chemical pesticide, DDT, caused them to lay eggs with no shells or shells so thin that they broke. By 1970, there was only one pair of nesting eagles in New Jersey. However, in 1972, DDT was banned and almost immediately populations of birds of prey began to recover.

In 1963, there were only 487 known pairs of nesting eagles in the lower 48 states. Today, there are nearly 10,000 pairs.

In New Jersey, there may be more than 150 active eagle nests, with many located by Delaware Bay, where eagles fish the open waters of the bay. In 2014, as many as 200 eagle chicks were born in the state.

Great horned owl

Peregrine falcons, whose population was similarly reduced by DDT, have also recovered. In the late 1970s, there were no active falcon nests in the state. Today, there may be 25 active nests.

Historically, falcons nested on cliffs and hunted birds and bats by diving on them from a great height. However, cliffs are no longer the nesting location of choice for these raptors. Instead, most nesting sites today are on tall buildings and bridges.

Many raptors have also been helped by changes in how land is used. A little more than a century ago, farm fields covered much of the Northeast, but many of those farms have been abandoned, and the fields have grown back to forests.

Today, the region has a rich mixture of landscapes – patches of forests that are alongside patches of meadows, farm fields or residential neighborhoods. And this change has helped many species, especially those that like to perch in trees on the edges of forests and hunt small animals in open areas, such as Cooper's hawks and red-tailed hawks.

However, a few species have been hurt by the changes, especially barn owls and northern harriers, which prefer farms and fields.

Red-tailed hawk nest

American kestrel

Broad-winged hawk

Barn owl

Osprey

Snowy owl

Raptors in flight

(Owls, which are generally nocturnal, are not usually seen in flight.)

Peregrine falcon

Bald eagle

Broad-winged hawk

American kestrel

Cooper's hawk

Northern harrier

Golden eagle

Northern goshawk

Red-shouldered hawk

Bald eagle

Buttermilk Falls near Layton in the Delaware Water Gap National Recreation Area

2–3 in. long

Graceful and elegant, deer are animals that a child might imagine in dreams. To see a doe and its fawns grazing in a meadow in the early morning light or an antlered buck nibbling tree seedlings in a sunlit forest is to see something that one does not easily forget.

But white-tailed deer graze in places other than meadows and forests. They graze in farm fields, in vegetable gardens and on ornamental shrubs. They also wander across well-traveled highways from dusk to dawn in search of still more grazing opportunities. And where deer go, Lyme disease, which is carried by deer ticks and which can affect humans, may follow. So not everyone loves to see whitetails.

A century ago, deer were rare in much of the Northeast. Sightings of them were often reported in newspapers. But with the return of the forests and limits on hunting, the deer also returned. By 2004, the size of the New Jersey's deer herd was estimated to be 204,000 animals. Today, with increased hunting, the population has been reduced to perhaps 110,000 animals. Nevertheless, there may still be 25,000 deer-vehicle collisions a year in New Jersey.

In the wild, white-tailed deer may live seven years or more. If food is plentiful, a doe may breed when she is six months old and have a fawn around her first birthday in the spring. In later years, she may have one to three fawns each spring, which means deer populations can grow rapidly.

As with many animals, the males are larger than the

White-tailed deer may gather in dense stands of evergreens, called "deer yards," in severe winters with deep snow. Snow depths are usually less there, and deer can browse on the branches. The trees also give them protection from wind, cold temperatures and blowing snow.

females. Bucks usually weigh 100 to 200 pounds, and does may reach 70 to 150 pounds. Bucks grow antlers each year, usually starting in April, and shed them in winter, late December to February.

There is a saying that when a leaf falls in the forest, an eagle will see it, a bear will smell it and a deer will hear it. Gifted with extremely sharp hearing, white-tailed deer are tough and hardy survivors. They use their hearing and swiftness afoot – they can run at speeds of 35 miles per hour – to avoid the few predators they have, and they can live close to residential neighborhoods while rarely being seen.

Deer prefer areas where there are forests mixed with clearings, wetlands, abandoned pastures or active farms. They are vegetarians, favoring the buds and twigs of young trees in the cold months, and grasses, fresh leaves and nuts, such as acorns, in the warm months.

White-tailed deer

6–7 in. long

What is there about a bear that has such a dramatic effect on people? From affection for panda bears to fear of grizzly bears, human emotions run high at the sight of them. Indeed, to come face-to-face with a bear is perhaps the ultimate wildlife experience of the forest – and increasingly of the suburbs.

Black bears were just about gone from the Garden State in 1900, pushed out mainly by unregulated hunting and trapping. As recently as the 1970s, New Jersey's bear population was estimated at fewer than 100 animals. Today, though, there may be 3,600 black bears roaming the state. And they have been sighted in all 21 of the state's counties.

In particular, northwestern New Jersey provides ideal bear habitat as its forests, thick with oaks, produce an abundance of acorns and other nuts – high on a bear's menu, especially in the fall, when it is trying to fatten up for winter in the den. A fatter female can produce larger and healthier litters during winter than one less well fed.

Black bears have long suffered from a public relations problem created by the larger, more aggressive grizzly bears, which are not found in the eastern United States. The difference is that eastern black bears rarely attack human beings. Usually, they are fairly docile creatures and won't attack unless they are defending a cub or have been surprised.

Black bears can live 25 years or more. Males typically weigh an average of 400 pounds, while females may weigh 185 pounds. Black bears have an extraordinary sense of smell that they use to locate food and detect danger. They eat little meat, focusing instead on plant matter that is available through the seasons, from skunk cabbage

Black bears are not true hibernators. While a bear's heart rate drops dramatically during the winter dormancy, its temperature does not. Female bears give birth to young in the den, typically in January, so a high body temperature is necessary for them to care for the young.

and grasses in the spring to apples and acorns in the fall. However, they may be drawn to backyard bird feeders and trash cans for easily obtained meals when other food supplies are lacking.

Black bears are usually active in daytime during the spring and fall, but they are more active during the hours around dawn and dusk in summer. They can run up to 35 miles per hour and are excellent swimmers and climbers.

Females give birth during their winter dormancy every other year, usually having two to four cubs.

Black bear cub scratching an itch

Black bear raiding a bird feeder

Black bear

*Red fox
track,
2 in. long*

To see a red fox in the wild is memorable. True to its reputation, a fox is as sly as ... well, a fox. Very secretive, it can live close to residential areas but almost never be seen. It's also an impressive looking animal with its silky red fur and sharp features.

Red foxes are not animals primarily of the deep forest. They prefer farmland or forest edges. The suburbs, with its mix of fields and small wood lots, can also be an excellent habitat for them.

By contrast, gray foxes, which are less common in New Jersey, usually live in forested or brushy areas.

Both red and gray foxes are smaller than most people expect, usually weighing just seven to 14 pounds, about as much as a large house cat. They have varied diets, eating what animals and plants are available through the seasons, including rabbits, rodents, birds, insects, snakes, turtles, apples and berries.

Gray fox

Red foxes are active year-round. In winter, they hunt small rodents, such as voles and mice, which move about in tunnels under the snow. A red fox's ears are very sensitive to low sounds, and it will sit on deep snow, listening for prey moving beneath it, then pounce, digging frantically, to capture the animal.

Very often, foxes will not eat what they capture, especially if they are full. Instead, they will bury the prey for a later meal.

Vixens, or female foxes, bear their young in dens in late March or early April. They may have four to seven kits, which begin to spend time outside the den in early May. By late summer, the young will leave their parents' care permanently.

Unlike red foxes, gray foxes, which have sharp claws, will climb trees to reach potential food, such as bird eggs or fruit. They will also scamper up a tree to escape danger and will jumnp from branch to branch. While a red fox den is nearly always underground, a gray fox will sometimes den off the ground in a hollow tree.

Red and gray foxes are found throughout New Jersey.

Red fox

Eastern coyote track, 2.5 in. long

"Ravenous cruell creatures." That was the description our Colonial ancestors gave of wolves.

Because of repeated attacks on their livestock, European settlers offered bounties for these stealthy predators, and gradually a predator that had been at the top of the food chain in the Northeast was eliminated.

It has long been assumed as fact that wolves no longer reside in the state. However, it now seems that assumption has been wrong – well, half wrong.

The wolf may again be on the prowl in New Jersey in the form of the eastern coyote. Genetic tests of tissue samples of coyotes in the Northeast have found evidence of wolf genes in the mix, sometimes to the point that the animals tested were more wolf than coyote.

Today, there are two wolves native to North America – the gray wolf, also called the timber wolf, which is found mainly in Canada, and the smaller, and more rare, red wolf. Only a few hundred red wolves remain and they live mainly in captivity in zoos and breeding facilities.

The eastern wolf, found mainly in eastern Canada, was thought to be a subspecies of gray wolf. However, some now believe it too may be a distinct species of wolf.

There had long been the suspicion that the eastern coyote had some wolf in it. It was known that coyotes, which were not found east of the Mississippi River

Eastern coyote

before 1900, migrated up into Canada from the western United States, crossed north of the Great Lakes and appeared in New Jersey in 1939, then spread east. However, this newly arrived coyote in the Northeast was noticeably larger than the coyote of the West. Did coyotes and wolves interbreed in Canada?

It took the rise of biotechnology and genetic analysis in the 1990s to confirm the suspicions. Indeed, researchers found wolf genes in eastern coyotes – mainly those of the eastern and gray wolves.

It is known that canids – members of the family that includes wolves, coyotes, foxes and dogs – will interbreed when mating partners of their own kind become scarce. And when so many wolves were killed when the continent was being colonized, wolfs apparently did mate with coyotes, producing our eastern coyote.

All this has thrown views of North America's "wild dogs" – wolves and coyotes – into a state of confusion. Some say the eastern coyote should more properly be called something else, perhaps even a new type of wolf.

Eastern coyotes are now found throughout the state, having been documented in all 21 counties.

Eastern coyote
Length: 4-5 ft.
(nose to tail)
Weight: 43 lbs.
(average male)

Western coyote
Length: 3.5-4.5 ft.
(nose to tail)
Weight: 33 lbs.
(average male)

Gray wolf
Length: 5-6 ft.
(nose to tail)
Weight: 80 lbs.
(average male)

Red wolf
Length: 4.5-5.5 ft.
(nose to tail)
Weight: 65 lbs.
(average male)

Eastern coyotes

The eastern coyote can look a lot like a German shepherd dog. However, coyotes are usually smaller and leaner. Also, a coyote's tail will usually be carried lower to the ground than that of a shepherd.

Eastern coyotes usually weigh 30 to 50 pounds, more than western coyotes. They are often grayish tan in color, but their coats can also be blond, red or even charcoal black. Strong swimmers, good jumpers (up to 15 feet) and swift runners (speeds of nearly 40 miles per hour have been observed), Eastern coyotes are also able hunters, with superior sight, smell and hearing.

Coyotes, which are most active from dusk to dawn, are usually no threat to humans. They are expert scavengers, eating almost anything edible from the bottom of the food chain to the top – from berries, fruits and insects to mice, rabbits and, yes, even the occasional house cat.

Eastern coyotes hunt alone, in mated pairs or in family groups. Coyotes are famous for their howls in the night, a form of communication for them. They will even howl in response to sirens, car alarms and train whistles. But often, the howling is meant to tell non-family members to stay out of the territory.

5 in. long

Beavers are nature's engineers, creating dams and lodges that are marvels of construction.

However, their dense, water-resistant fur has always been highly prized for clothing, and uncontrolled trapping during Colonial times eliminated beavers from much of the Northeast.

Virtually trapped out of New Jersey and much of the Northeast by the late 1700s, beavers have slowly moved back into many areas of the state, helped by a regulated trapping season and wildlife restoration programs. However, they are most common in rural areas of the state where there is a constant source of water.

But as the beaver population grows and spreads, these industrious animals often compete for space in residential areas. Having a beaver pond in the neighborhood is a delight to many people, but a nuisance to others as the ponds can sometimes flood back yards, roads and wells.

From their protruding, orange-tinted, buck teeth to the end of their paddlelike tails, adult beavers are two to three feet long, and they can weigh 30 to 70 pounds. They use their broad, flat tails as rudders when they swim, but they also use them to warn other beavers of danger by loudly slapping them on the water's surface. A beaver can stay submerged in water for up to 15 minutes.

Beavers use trees as their prime building material, and they also feed on the bark. Their favorite trees include poplars, birches, maples, willows and alders. They usually fell trees at night and are able to gnaw their way through a willow that is five inches in diameter in just a few minutes.

Beavers dam streams to create ponds. They spend much of their lives in water, which protects them from preda-

A beaver lodge

Plunge hole   Dry platform   Water level inside the lodge   Dam

tors. They begin by laying branches and twigs across a stream that may be in a slight valley. Then they pack down this material with mud, extending the dam's width and height as they go.

Their trademark lodge can sit near the shore of a pond or right in the middle, surrounded by water. The roof of the lodge is made of twigs and mud. Inside, it has a dry platform just above the water line with one or two plunge holes for an entrance and exit. For protection, beavers almost always work on dams and lodges at night.

In winter, beavers do not hibernate. They remain awake in the lodge, occasionally going out beneath the ice to retrieve tree branches they've stored in the water nearby for a meal. A family of beavers can eat a ton of bark in winter.

Beavers take a mate for life. The young, called kits, are born in May or June and will take to the water within hours.

Once they dam a stream, a family of beavers typically stays in that location five or six years, expanding the system of dams and ponds as the family grows. Several generations of the family can make up the colony.

A beaver lodge

A beaver and a freshly gnawed tree

A beaver's strong orange teeth

1.5 in. long

A blood-curdling scream deep in the night brings frantic calls to local police, but no evidence of any kind of crime is found.

The mystery is no mystery to wildlife biologists. They know that in the spring what may sound like a crime of passion is in many cases a bobcat in the heat of passion during mating. Its scream is similar in pitch to that of a human female.

Sly. Secretive. Solitary. Bobcats are a rare sight even in areas where they might be common. Bobcats may look like house cats who have done some serious weight training, but the two have quite different lineages. House cats are descended from the first cats domesticated about 4,000 years ago, when Egyptians took the African wild cat and tamed it to keep granaries free of rodents. Later, they were bred as pets.

Bobcats, on the other hand, derive from the Eurasian lynx that took the opportunity perhaps two million years ago to migrate from Asia to North America across a periodic land bridge that emerged across the Bering Strait during ice ages. The lynx learned to live in snow-free regions of the continent, including Mexico, and eventually evolved into the more muscular bobcat.

Visually, what distinguishes the bobcat from most house cats is its tail. It's a bobbed, or shortened, version, about six inches long, of what one usually sees on the house cat. The way a bobcat carries itself can also tell you this is not a house cat on the prowl. They have a certain confidence, a sense that they are only predator and not prey

The bobcat is listed as an endangered species in New Jersey, although the size of its population is unknown since they are secretive and difficult to survey. They are most common in the state's northern counties.

Typically, bobcats are 28 to 47 inches long and weigh 15 to 35 pounds. Females have one litter per year of one to four kittens born in spring. The young are raised entirely by the female as the male takes no part in family life.

Bobcats, which live about 12 years on average in the wild, are active before dusk to just after dawn in summer and also during the daytime in winter. Their dens are usually formed in a rock crevice, cave, brush pile or hollow log and then lined with dried grass, leaves, moss,

Bobcats will capture an animal, such as a young or sick deer, in winter and eat until they are full. Then they will cover the carcass with snow to return to later for a meal.

and other soft vegetation. They are active throughout the year.

Their diet consists of rabbits and other small mammals in summer, and in winter, snowshoe hares, if they can find them, and occasionally sick or weakened deer. For younger bobcats, starvation is the number one killer.

Bobcat

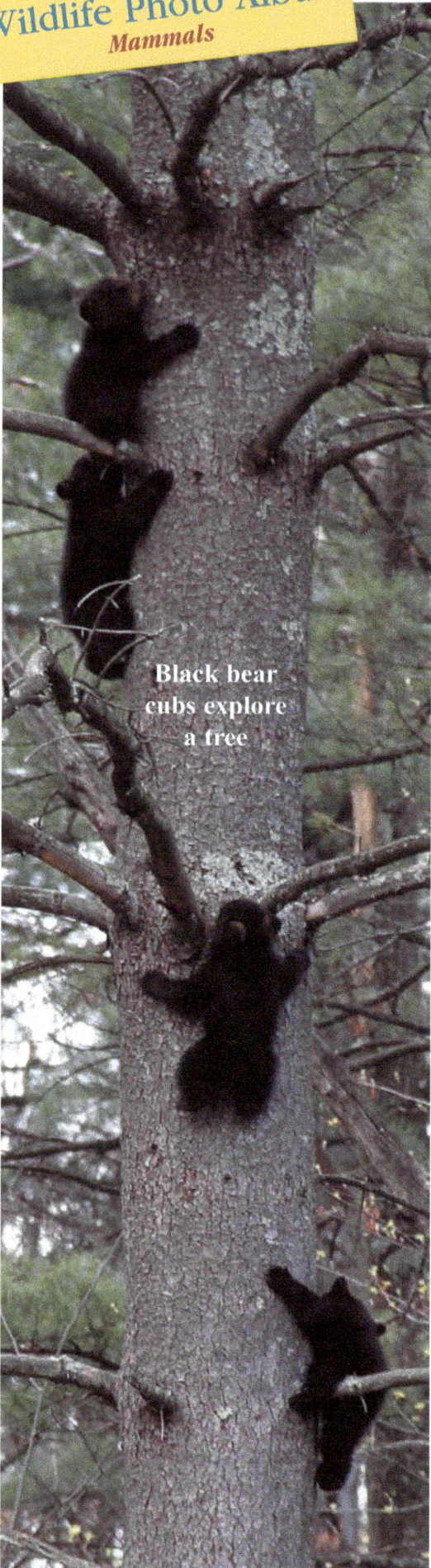

Black bear cubs explore a tree

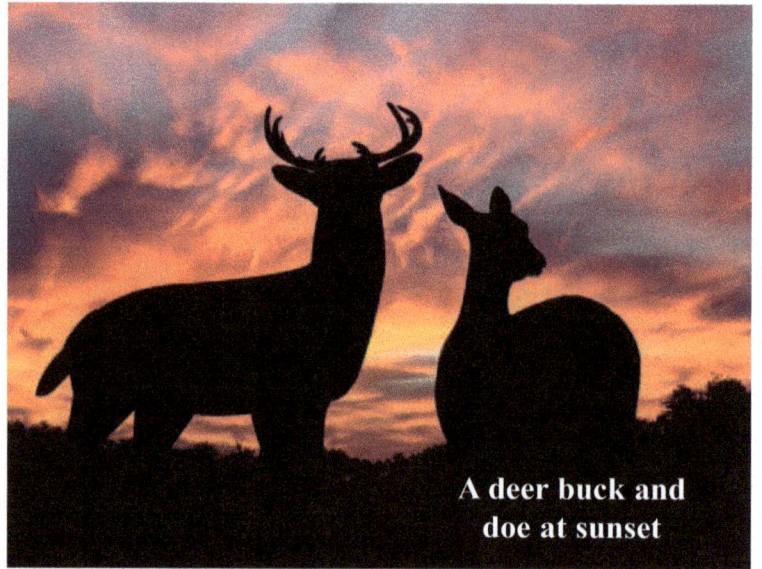

A deer buck and doe at sunset

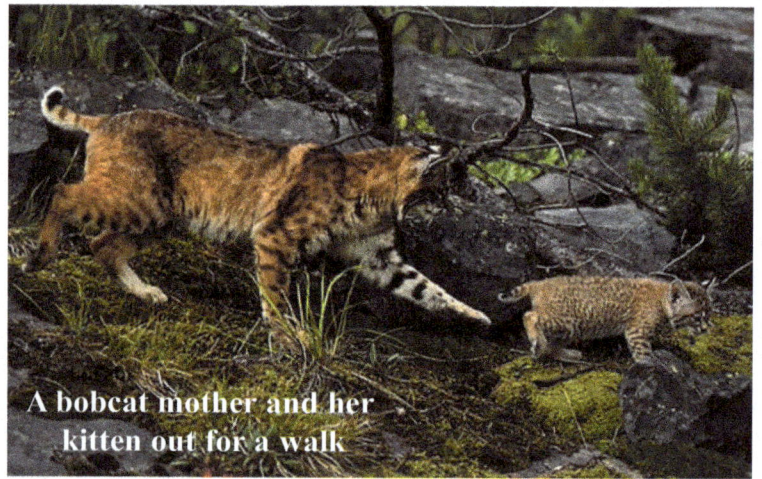

A bobcat mother and her kitten out for a walk

A raccoon hunts in a wetland

A young porcupine practices climbing

Red fox kits emerge from their den

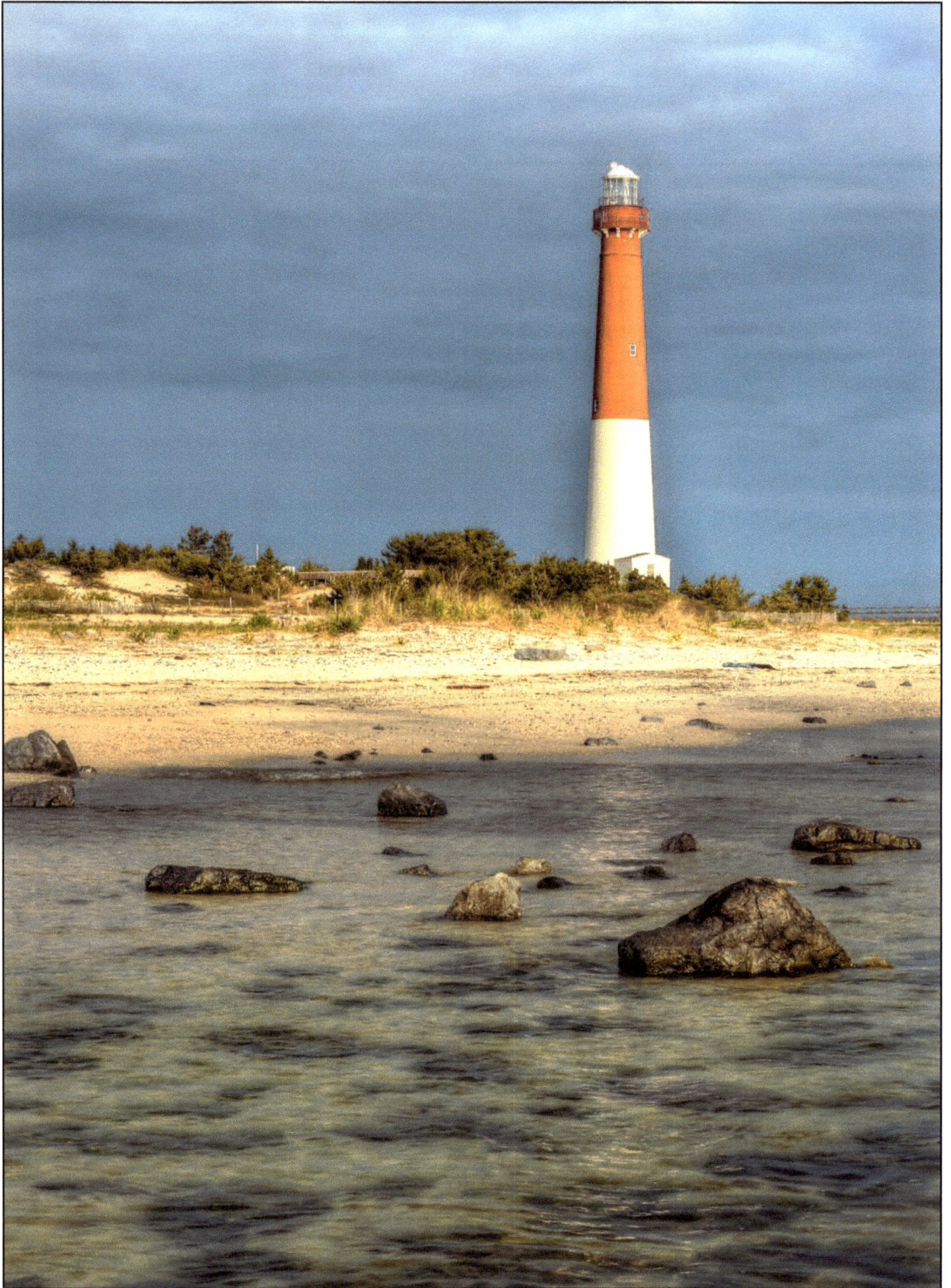
Barnegat Lighthouse on Long Beach Island in Ocean County

Bald eagles, Bengal tigers and giant pandas are all darlings of science and the media, sharing a charisma factor. Bats, along with cockroaches and rats, suffer from a "yuck" factor and are largely shunned.

However, there would be a world of difference in a world without bats. They eat an amazing number of insects, primarily moths and beetles. It's estimated that a single bat can eat 600 insects in an hour (although contrary to popular belief, mosquitoes are not a principal part of a bat's diet).

We may soon experience a world without bats, though. In New Jersey and elsewhere bats are dying in high numbers. A fungus, called white-nose syndrome, is threatening bats throughout the eastern United States and Canada, causing devastating losses of their populations.

Once the most common bat in the United States, the little brown bat is now being considered for the endangered species list. It's estimated that nearly 95 percent of little brown bats in the eastern half of the country have died from white-nose syndrome.

First identified in New York in 2006, the disease has spread rapidly. As of 2014, it had been detected in bats in 25 states in the eastern United States and in five Canadian provinces. Some scientists believe the little brown bat may vanish from the country entirely in a little more than a decade.

Often described as "flying mice," bats are, in fact, not rodents. They are mammals. There are nine species of bats that are native to New Jersey, including the two most common, the little and big brown bats. The little brown bat has about a 10-inch wingspan while the big brown bat measures 13 inches wing tip to wing tip. Typically, a little brown bat weighs just a quarter of an ounce, about the weight of a quarter, compared to two-thirds of an ounce for the big brown bat.

Prior to the current bat illness, the little brown bat was the species most people crossed paths with, as it has a habit of slipping into houses through impossibly small gaps and holes. In summer, during the day. the little brown may roost, or rest, in attics, behind window shutters and in other dark, hot, sheltered places.

While bats can be carriers of rabies, they are not usually infected. But health officials warn people never to handle

A bat's radar

Bats have fairly good eyesight, but in the dark, eyes have little value. So bats have evolved to have a kind of radar that depends on high-frequency sounds that humans can't hear. As a bat flies, it emits short cries at this frequency. The waves of sound go out and when they hit something solid, such as a tree branch or a flying insect, they bounce off the object and return to the bat, which picks up the returning sound with its ears. The bat's brain analyzes the time the sound wave took to return, whether it is an irregular signal and what its pitch is to determine how far ahead the object is. These things will tell it whether it is a flying insect, and whether or not it is moving toward the bat or away from it. For instance, the fluttering wings of a moth might produce a fluttering echo wave.

Echo wave

a bat with bare hands and to treat any bat flying in the living quarters of a home as if it has rabies. The best method to get rid of it is to open a window and leave the room.

The bats in New Jersey have two main wintering strategies. The hoary, red and silver-haired bats migrate south with the birds. All of the others go to mines and caves in September and October to hibernate.

Why mines and caves? In winter, the temperature and humidity in these chambers can be considerably higher than conditions outside. During hibernation for little brown bats, breathing slows to one breath every five minutes and body temperature drops until it is only slightly higher than the surrounding air. Groups of them form tight clusters, hanging from the ceiling by their feet.

It is in these hibernating chambers that white-nose syndrome spreads within these large groups of sleeping bats. One of the largest hibernation sites in the state has been the Hibernia Mine in Rockaway Township. Prior to the outbreak of the disease, it attracted as many as 30,000 little brown bats in winter. A count in March of 2015 found 462 bats.

Little brown bat

1.5 in. long

"Once bitten, twice shy" certainly applies to those who have encountered striped skunks. Sprayed just once with a striped skunk's unmistakable scent, and you will never want to repeat the experience.

Skunks have one of the more effective defenses against predators on the planet. Their scent spray, which can travel 15 feet in the air if the wind is right, is so strong it can temporarily blind a victim.

Their bold coloring – black with a white stripe running down their back – makes the lesson that much more unforgettable. "If you see another animal that looks like this, stay clear," the distinctive colors seem to say.

Skunks, which usually weigh three to 12 pounds, eat almost anything, including snails, small rodents, birds' eggs, fruit, grain, nuts, berries and garbage.

Typically, they are nocturnal animals. A sign one has been in your yard is shallow holes dug in the ground. A skunk was likely digging for grubs or worms during the night.

Skunks are usually active earlier in the spring than other mammals. They might spend the winter under a stump, in a stone wall, in an abandoned burrow or even under a house. But in mid-February the breeding season starts. Males may emerge from their dens and travel in search of females even when there is snow on the ground. This is a time of year when wandering males often cross paths with dogs, coyotes and other non-hibernating species. For many people, the pungent odor that results from such a meeting is one of the first signs that spring is on the way.

Striped skunks usually do not spray without warning. Here's what to look for if you find yourself face-to-face with a skunk. When confronted, a skunk will usually face you, raise its tail, chatter its teeth and stomp the ground with its front feet. If this doesn't send you in retreat, it will then twist its rear end toward you while still facing you, and discharge its spray in your direction. There may be enough spray in reserve for four or five discharges. If the skunk scores a direct hit, don't even bother washing your clothes. Just throw them away.

The scent itself is composed of a compound containing sulfur that is secreted by the anal glands. In fact, skunks can be relatively gentle animals and typically will not discharge their scent except as a last resort.

Home remedies to remove the scent from skunk-doused pets often mention a bath in tomato juice, beer or vinegar. But studies have found a more effective mixture is one quart of three percent hydrogen peroxide (which can be obtained from a drug store), a quarter cup of baking soda (sodium bicarbonate) and a teaspoon of liquid detergent. This mixture chemically neutralizes the scent rather than just covering it up.

Skunks are common throughout New Jersey.

Striped skunk

Gray squirrel track, 2.5 in. long

The squirrel is one of nature's bankers, wisely putting away resources for the future. Each fall, eastern gray squirrels go about collecting nuts (their favorite food) and burying them one by one for the time when the snow falls and their sources of food disappear.

When winter arrives, they can find their stores, or caches, of acorns and other nuts, sometimes beneath a foot of snow. It's believed they are able to do this through a combination of memory and smell.

Squirrels are rodents, as are chipmunks, woodchucks, beavers and mice. Most rodents hoard or store food to some extent.

In New Jersey, eastern gray squirrels are the squirrels most commonly seen by people. With their quickness and ability to move acrobatically through the treetops, gray squirrels live easily around people and can thrive in residential areas with trees.

Red squirrels are common in many areas with evergreen trees, including residential neighborhoods. However, southern and northern flying squirrels are natives of the state but uncommon.

Gray squirrels may have two litters each year, usually of two to four young per litter. One litter may be born in March and another in July or August. The spring litter is born in a tree den, which is a hollow cavity in a live

Flying squirrels

don't actually fly and they don't have wings. They spread open flaps of loose skin between their front and rear legs and glide through the air. Glides of up to 50 yards have been observed.

Southern flying squirrel

tree also used during winter for shelter. The summer litter may be born in a large nest built high in a tree using leaves and sticks. When the leaves fall in autumn, these large nests become visible, looking like massive bird nests.

From its nose to the tip of its tail, the gray squirrel is typically 18 to 20 inches long, while the red squirrel is 12 to 14 inches long and the two flying squirrels are nine to 11 inches in length.

Squirrels use their long bushy tails for shade, warmth, protection from rain and snow, balance when climbing and communication with other squirrels. A flying squirrel will also use its tail as a brake and rudder in flight.

Although squirrels may stay in their dens for several days at a time when the weather is harsh in winter, they are active throughout the year.

Eastern gray squirrel

Red squirrel

Yes, there are bears and deer in the woods, but it is the small critters that really populate the great outdoors.

In a square mile of good habitat, there might be a few red foxes, a few dozen striped skunks, a few hundred eastern chipmunks and a few thousand short-tailed shrews. That's not to mention the brown bats, red squirrels, gray foxes, beavers, porcupines, cottontails, weasels, coyotes, woodchucks, otters, fishers, bobcats, muskrats, rabbits, voles, mice, minks and moles.

But if there are that many mammals out there, why do we see so few? The reason is that many species are secretive and have habits that help them avoid predators (and human beings). For instance, many are nocturnal – active mainly at night. They sleep and rest in hidden places by day but then go out foraging for food once the sun goes down.

With so many animals sharing the same land, many have evolved to be specialists in where they live and what they eat so that they can survive despite the competition.

Muskrats, beavers and river otters spend much of their life in water. Shrews, moles and voles spend much of their life underground or under the cover of thick grasses or leaves. Squirrels and porcupines spend most of their time in trees. And bats fly.

Porcupines, rabbits and woodchucks are vegetarians. Moles eat worms and ground insects. Bats eat flying insects. Skunks, raccoons and opossums will eat almost anything that can be eaten, including garbage.

Even among mammals, though, there are predators and prey, roles that are often determined by size. The shrews, mice, voles and moles tend to be the

Eastern cottontail

Porcupine

prey, while the foxes, coyotes and bobcats are often the predators.

When approached by a predator, prey animals will use their specialized defenses. The opossum can act as if it's dead. The eastern cottontail can leap 15 feet. Snowshoe hares, which turn white in winter and blend with the snow, can run 27 miles per hour. Striped skunks can spray a fluid that smells terrible and can cause temporary blindness. Porcupines can protect themselves with their coat of sharp quills – as many as 30,000 needle-like spines.

In winter, many mammals either hibernate or become inactive in their dens or burrows. But some, such as coyotes and foxes, are active throughout the year.

It is not just the deep woods and rural meadows that are home to so many mammals. Even urban and suburban neighborhoods can be teeming with wild animals, and not just mammals. Many snakes, birds and insects also call this kind of habitat home.

Because many mammals, such as opossums and skunks, are nocturnal, you rarely see them in residential areas. But they're there. Ask any policeman who drives a cruiser on the midnight to dawn shift.

In fact, when an area is transformed from a rural to a residential landscape, some animals find life easier. They learn to adapt their diet to the new opportunities these neighborhoods can offer, such as bird feeders, vegetable gardens, trash cans, and healthy lawns and shrubs.

Many animals, such as squirrels, chipmunks and a variety of birds, live comfortably with people and are often in sight. Other animals, including garter snakes and woodchucks, live easily among people but prefer to stay out of sight as much as possible.

Raccoon

River otter

Opossum

Woodchuck (groundhog)

Muskrat

Chipmunk

River otter

35 to 54 in. – 12 to 20 lbs. – One litter per year of two to four young born March or April – Active mainly from dusk to after dawn, but can be active any time of day – Eats primarily fish, but also frogs, turtles and aquatic insects – Dens in a rock crevice, under a fallen tree, in an abandoned beaver lodge or muskrat house or in thickets beside water – Active throughout the year

3 in. wide

Porcupine

24 to 30 in. – 8 to 20 lbs. – One litter per year of one young born April to June – Active mainly at night – A strict vegetarian, it eats grasses, twigs, buds and bark – Most den in winter in rocky fissures, hollow trees and logs or vacant buildings, such as sheds, but they may emerge to feed during the day – Active throughout the year

3 in. long

Muskrat

2 in. long

19 to 25 in. (half its length is its tail) – 1 to 4 lbs. – Two to four litters per year of three to eight young born April to September – Active mainly at night, but may be seen during the day – Eats mainly aquatic plants, such as cattails and pond weeds – Constructs a lodge of weeds on water or digs a den in a stream bank – Active throughout the year

1 in. long

Chipmunk

8 to 10 in. – 2 to 5 oz. – One litter per year of three to five young born in April or May – Active all times of day – Eats mainly seeds, fruits, nuts and insects – Dens underground in a series of tunnels – Hibernates in winter, but may become active for short periods

Opossum

26 to 35 in. – 5 to 9 lbs. – One or two litters per year usually of six to nine young, but sometimes as many as 20, born February to July – Active mainly at night – Eats nearly anything, including insects, fruits, nuts, carrion and garbage – Dens in an abandoned burrow, tree cavity, brush pile or thicket – Becomes less active in winter, but does not hibernate

2.5 in. wide

Eastern cottontail

14 to 18 in. – 2 to 4 lbs. – Three to seven litters per year of three to six young – Most active dusk to just after dawn – Eats mainly plant matter, such as grasses and herbs, in summer, and bark, twigs and buds in winter – Finds shelter year-round in brush piles, stone walls or abandoned dens and burrows – Active year-round

3-4 in. long

3.5 in. long

Raccoon

22 to 34 in. – 15 to 25 lbs. – One litter per year of three to seven young born April or May – Active mainly at night – Eats everything from small animals and birds to grains and garbage – Dens in a ground cavity, hollow tree, hollow log, pile of rubbish, attic or chimney – Spends winters in its den, but does not hibernate

2 in. long

Woodchuck

19 to 27 in. – 4 to 14 lbs. – One litter per year of four to six young born early April to mid-May – Active by day, especially in the early morning and late afternoon – Eats mainly plants, such as clover and grasses – Dens in a series of underground tunnels ending in a chamber with a grass nest – Hibernates in winter

Roadkill is one of those grisly facts of life.

But to many naturalists, what lies in repose by the roadside can be a source of valuable information if not general fascination. For instance, why do some animals regularly end up as highway fatalities and others do not? As agile as squirrels are, why are they so often victimized? And how is it that fragile little sparrows, which spend so much time down on the roadway, don't even make the list of top 10 road-killed birds (yes, there is such a list), yet the more reclusive gray catbird is right up there among the leaders?

It is unfortunate, but the carnage on the nation's highways is breathtaking. By some estimates, as many as a million animals meet their demise in traffic daily. It may be moose in Maine, white-tailed deer in Pennsylvania, armadillos in Arizona, rattlesnakes in Texas or whiptail lizards in New Mexico.

One survey by a Massachusetts naturalist chronicled roadkill, some 4,000 dead animals, the researcher spotted along the state's highways from 1985 to 1991. To no one's surprise, gray squirrels topped the list. Among birds, pigeons, which often nest beneath overpasses, were the number one victim.

A crow feeds on a road-killed squirrel

Part of the explanation for why squirrels so frequently expire on highways is the sheer number of squirrels. However, part of the explanation may also be the strange mind of the squirrel. It may go half way across a road, see a car, and dart back right under the wheels.

Among road-killed mammals in the survey (which did not include domestic cats and dogs), the numbers went like this: 1,488 gray squirrels, 445 opossums, 270 raccoons (before the current raccoon rabies outbreak that began in New York in 1990), 196 striped skunks, 194 cottontail rabbits, 111 woodchucks, 100 chipmunks, 77 muskrats and 56 red squirrels.

Although residents of the air, birds nearly always end their lives on the ground, many of them on the highways of America. (A few are plucked from midair by predatory birds.) The survey included 1,000 road-killed birds, and it found 166 pigeons, 163 robins (they tend to fly low across the road), 80 starlings, 75 blue jays, 65 gray catbirds (another low flyer), 62 grackles, 41 flickers (a fatal attraction to ants), 33 eastern screech owls (they chase flying insects), 32 crows (they scavenge roadkill) and 31 mourning doves.

Why aren't chipping and house sparrows, ever-present on road shoulders, high on the list? Perhaps it is just good instincts and maneuverability.

Then there is the question of what becomes of roadkill. In many communities, highway crews remove the remains. But often, nature supplies its own cleanup crew, from microscopic bacteria to scavengers as large as turkey vultures. Crows, raccoons, coyotes and even an occasional red-tailed hawk also feed in traffic.

Turkey vultures

The undertakers of the air, turkey vultures may spend most of the day soaring in the sky, searching for food using both their eyesight and keen sense of smell. The odor they are seeking is ethyl mercaptan, a chemical created by rotting meat.

However, circling vultures do not necessarily mean there is a dead animal below. The birds could just be traveling higher on a thermal, a rising column of warm air. Riding these thermals, a turkey vulture with a wingspan of about six feet can glide for as much as six hours without once

beating its wings.

Turkey vultures feed on dead animals. They will not circle or stalk a dying or healthy animal. However, plant matter is also a part of their diet.

The males and females are identical in appearance. Both have a bald red head (like a turkey).

The reason it is bald is that when a turkey vulture is feeding, it may have to stick its head into the carcass to find meat, and if there were feathers on its head, they would catch bits of the animal, including any parasites or bacteria it might harbor.

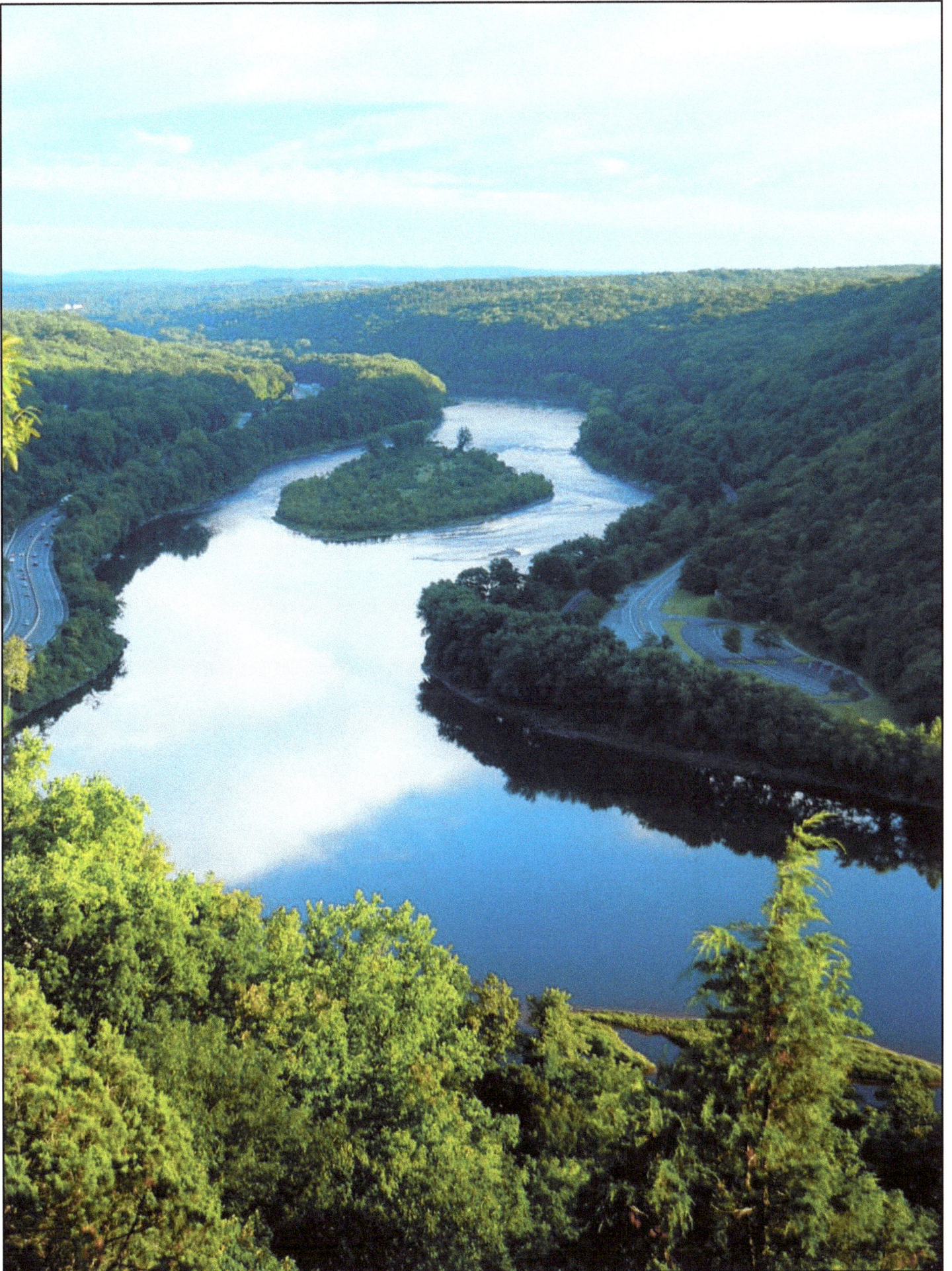

The Delaware River, looking south, as it passes through the Delaware Water Gap
between New Jersey, on the left, and Pennsylvania, on the right

Garter snakes may have 40 of them, opossums usually have about eight, catbirds often have four, and bats and porcupines have just one.

What are they? They're offspring. And different species of animals may have very different numbers of young when they become parents.

There are other differences as well in the reproductive habits of animals. Birds, butterflies and frogs lay eggs, but mammals, such as foxes, chipmunks and bears, have live young. Turtles may never meet their mothers, deer fawns may stay with their mothers nearly a year, and crows may stay together as a family composed of several generations.

But like most things that animals do, there is a purpose and a plan to the way they raise their families.

Frequently in their development, species face choices. To best ensure that a species survives, does it have a lot of young or just a few? Does it spend a lot of time taking care of the offspring or very little?

For instance, if a mother has lots of young each season, the chances are greater that some will survive to adulthood so they too can have families and keep the species alive. However, if she does have lots of young, she will have a harder time feeding them than if she has just a few babies. So which approach is best for species survival?

Animals do not consciously choose to use one approach or another. Essentially, life makes the decision for them. Let's say there is a species of animal in which litter size varies greatly. Some mothers have the biological trait – the genes – for having small litters, and some have the genes for large litters. But let's say that because of a permanent change in the availability of food, the young from small litters are more likely to survive. These young would inherit the genes for small litters from their parents, and when they get to be parents, they will have small litters too. In not too many generations, most families of this species may be having small litters, and large litters might disappear completely.

If a species has been around a long time, chances are its method of reproduction has worked well. It is probably right for its situation.

For instance, birds need to be light to fly, and they need to eat a lot of food in comparison to their weight in order to have the energy to fly. They might have had a hard time surviving if they did not lay eggs. A mother bird might weigh too much to fly and feed if she were carrying her young inside her as they developed. She might also be more vulnerable to predators. So eggs that develop and hatch outside a mother's body are a good solution for birds.

Sometimes different approaches to reproduction work just as well. Some snakes, such as garter snakes, have live young, while others, such as milk snakes, lay eggs. The fact that snakes using each method are common seems to indicate neither method has a clear advantage for snakes.

Spring is the time for most offspring. Baby red foxes, woodchucks and river otters might be born just as spring starts. Mallards often lay eggs in April that hatch in May. Bobcats, skunks and chipmunks might have their young in May. Most songbirds, such as northern cardinals and tree sparrows, lay their eggs in May and June. Deer and little brown bats might be born in June.

For animals that are cared for by their parents, how long they remain in the nest or den varies by species. But as a general rule, the larger an animal is, the longer it will stay in the care of its parents.

Deer fawn

Red fox kit

An American goldfinch feeding its young

Bobcat kitten

The birds and the bees: Family planning in the animal kingdom

PAINTED TURTLE – From three to 14 eggs are laid in a hole dug on land in late spring, then the mother leaves the nest permanently. The eggs take about 75 days to hatch, then the young find water on their own.

GREEN FROG – As many as 4,000 eggs are laid in jelly-like masses in water, typically in mid-spring. The eggs hatch in three to six days, and the young may spend a year as tadpoles before changing into frogs.

HONEY BEE – The queen bee may lay up to 2,000 eggs a day and 200,000 eggs a season. An egg develops in a wax cell in the hive's brood area, hatching in about three days.

RED-TAILED HAWK – Typically, two or three eggs are laid in a stick nest built high in a tall tree. The eggs hatch in about a month. The young take first flights about 45 days later.

MEADOW VOLE – Also called field mice, these small mammals may have as many as 10 litters of live young a year, and there may be up to nine young per litter. The young may spend only two weeks being fed by their mother before they are on their own.

GARDEN SPIDER – Hundreds of eggs are laid in a sac on a leaf, twig or a support in the fall. The mother dies when the weather turns cold and the spiderlings overwinter in the egg sac.

WHITE-TAILED DEER – Usually two fawns are born in late May or early June. They feed on their mother's milk for about three weeks, then they begin to browse on vegetation. Males may leave their mothers by the fall. Females may stay with them up to two years.

RACCOON – Typically, three to seven young are born in a hollow tree in April or May. The young, which have the characteristic mask of raccoons soon after birth, venture from the den in about seven weeks to run and climb.

PUMPKINSEED – Using his fins, the male carves out a saucer-shaped nest in sand or gravel in shallow water in May or June. The female lays 1,700 or more eggs that hatch in as little as three days.

GARTER SNAKE – Females give birth to live young. The litter, delivered between July and September, may number 14 to 40 young. The newborns are immediately on their own.

Baby skunk

Magnolia warblers in their nest

What do you do if you find a baby animal?

You're walking through a field and come across a baby fawn standing motionless and alone in the tall grass. You find a baby bird beneath a tree in your back yard and there's no sign of either parent nearby. You accidentally uncover a nest of baby rabbits in thick grass on the edge of a lawn. What do you do?

Wildlife officials like to say, "If you care, leave them there."

In the majority of cases, an animal that appears to be orphaned really isn't. The mother may have wandered off in search of food, or she may be close by, waiting for you to leave. However, it may be that a young animal is out on its own. In the first days that animals leave the nest or den, they learn valuable lessons about finding food and protecting themselves that they will never have the chance to learn if you take them in without a good reason.

If the baby animal is truly abandoned or if you see an animal, baby or adult, that is obviously injured, call a veterinarian, an animal control officer or a licensed wildlife rehabilitator. If it's in your back yard, keep pet cats and dogs away while you wait.

If you decide it is necessary and safe to handle the animal, wear thick gloves and put it in a box with air holes and material, such as leaves or grass, on the bottom so that the animal does not slide around. Handle it as little as possible and call a wildlife officer.

However, it's not true that a mother animal will reject a baby if it has been touched by a human. She will take it back.

Most important, if the animal seems agitated or aggressive, do not handle it. Mammals, such as raccoons, foxes, skunks and bats, can carry rabies, a dangerous disease that can be passed to humans through an infected animal's saliva.

Milk snake

Snakes can awaken primitive fears in us. The sudden discovery of a snake sunning itself on the front walk or slithering through the garden is enough to startle almost anyone.

But despite the impressive size of some native snakes of New Jersey (the black rat snake can reach a length of up to eight feet), the chance of encountering one that could truly do you harm is very small. Of the 22 species of snakes that are native to the state, only two are venomous – the timber rattlesnake and the northern copperhead. They were both hunted with great intensity over the centuries, reducing their populations to the point that the timber rattlesnake is an endangered species and the copperhead is a species of special concern in New Jersey. They are usually found in remote spots in the state, places humans rarely inhabit, such as high on rocky mountainsides or deep within large forests.

Snakes live everywhere in New Jersey. You're most likely to see a snake in the spring, when it is out of hibernation and basking in the sun. And the snake you're most likely to see is the garter snake, the most common snake in the state. Many snakes, such as the black racer, lay eggs, but others, such as the garter snake, have live young.

The northern water snake is the next most common

Northern copperhead

Ringneck snake

snake in the state. A harmless snake, it is frequently mistaken for the poisonous water moccasin, also called the cottonmouth. However, there are no water moccasins north of Virginia.

The damage from being bitten by a non-venomous snake is more psychological than physical. The wound is typically no more serious than being scratched by a thorn of a rosebush.

New Jersey's most abundant venomous snake, the northern copperhead is found only in the northern counties.

The timber rattlesnake is the larger of the two venomous snakes native to the state, typically reaching three to four feet in length. It hunts mainly at night and is most active on nights with a full moon when it will wait in ambush for prey like chipmunks, squirrels or rabbits. It

Garter snake

New Jersey's snakes
(Average length of snakes that are either common or venomous)

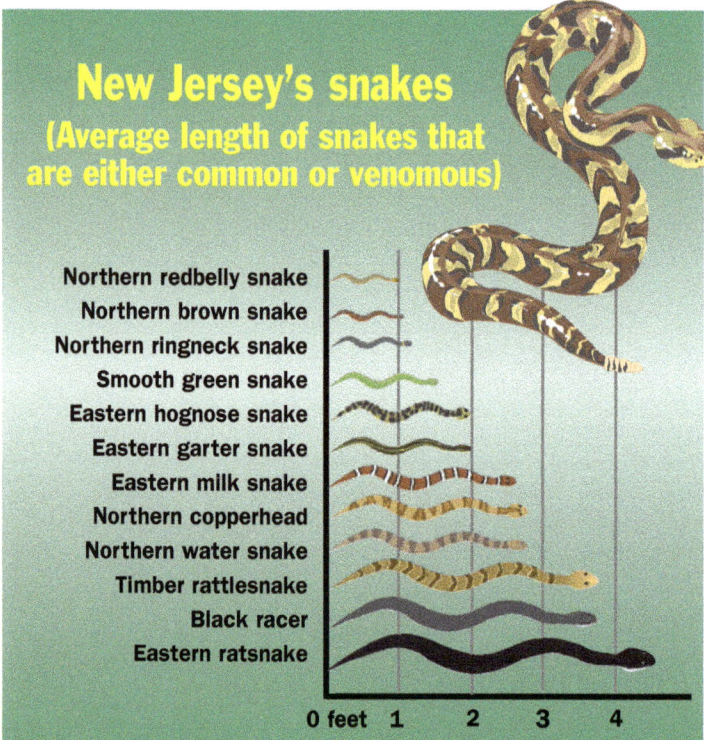

	0 feet	1	2	3	4
Northern redbelly snake					
Northern brown snake					
Northern ringneck snake					
Smooth green snake					
Eastern hognose snake					
Eastern garter snake					
Eastern milk snake					
Northern copperhead					
Northern water snake					
Timber rattlesnake					
Black racer					
Eastern ratsnake					

Smooth green snake

will then lunge at the animal, dig in its fangs, inject its venom, then withdraw to wait for the animal to die, which usually takes just a few minutes. If the animal is able to wander off, the rattlesnake will track it down by scent. It will then try to swallow the dead animal whole. Copperheads and timber rattlesnakes may eat only a dozen meals a year.

The timber rattlesnake is found in the northern counties and within the pine barrens of south-central New Jersey.

Smaller snakes usually search for insects, slugs, earthworms or frogs for their meals. Larger snakes may also hunt small rodents and birds.

All snakes swallow their prey whole, usually seizing the animal first with their jaws. Their upper and lower jaws are not connected, allowing some snakes to open their mouth wide enough to swallow prey larger than their head. However, a few snakes, including the black rat snake and milk snake, may firsy wrap their body around the prey and squeeze it to make the kill.

Black rat snake

Some snakes, such as the milk snake and black racer, will vibrate their tails as a display to scare away predators. People often mistake this for the rattle of a timber rattlesnake. But the rattlesnake has a very distinct rattle on it that when shaken sounds almost like a baby's toy rattle.

In winter, snakes in the Northeast hibernate in burrows or hollows or even in holes in the foundations of homes.

Most snakes are hatched or born in the summer, and they are left on their own to find food from the start. As snakes grow, they periodically shed their outer skin – like throwing away an old set of clothes – because they outgrow it. This is called shedding or molting.

Timber rattlesnake

Box turtle, 4 to 8.5 in.

Snapping turtle, 8 to 19 in.

Nature does not fix what isn't broken. Despite being slower and more awkward than almost any other animal its size or larger, turtles have changed remarkably little since they first appeared nearly 220 million years ago, well before most dinosaurs. Their basic design – a soft body contained inside a hard shell – has worked very well for them, providing them excellent protection against predators. In fact, some turtles may live 100 years or more.

The chief threat to turtles is humans. Many turtles are disappearing from the wild because they are collected for the pet trade. Some species are vanishing because their nesting sites, the places where they go to lay eggs, have been developed for businesses and homes.

Like snakes, turtles are reptiles, which means they cannot warm their bodies from the inside the way humans and other mammals do. Instead, reptiles must take action to warm up. For instance, they can bask in the sun. On cool spring days or on summer mornings, you will often see turtles in ponds doing just this, as they sit on top of logs or rocks.

Turtles have no teeth. They use their hard bills to scissor apart their food. In water, they eat aquatic insects, fish, frogs and plants. On land, earthworms, snails, grasshoppers, fruits and berries are all part of their diet.

A turtle's shell is both its mobile home and its protection. The top part of the shell, called the carapace, is attached to the turtle's backbone. The lower half of the shell is called the plastron. Despite what you see in cartoons, turtles cannot leave their shells. The box turtle has a hinge on its plastron so that when it pulls in its head and legs to escape a predator the shell closes up, leaving almost no flesh visible.

Turtles have lungs but no gills. Some are able to breathe underwater by absorbing oxygen from the water through their exposed skin. In winter, many turtles settle down into the mud at the bottom of ponds or rivers to hibernate. Land turtles, such as the box turtle, dig beneath soft dirt or decaying leaves to hibernate.

Worldwide, there are nearly 320 species of turtles. Thirteen species can be found in New Jersey. The most common turtle found in the state is the painted turtle. It lives almost anywhere there are bodies of fresh water.

Snapping turtles, which spend most of their time underwater, are the largest inland turtles found in the state, but they are rarely seen except during the breeding season when they come onto land from ponds and lakes to lay eggs.

One of the rarest and smallest turtles (about 3.5 inches in length) in North America is the bog turtle. In New Jersey, where it is endangered, it occurs in agricultural areas of the northwestern and southwestern parts of the state.

The diamondback terrapin is the only turtle in the state that can be found in saltwater environments, such as coastal marshes, estuaries and barrier beach lagoons.

Turtles all lay eggs in the ground. Even a turtle that spends nearly all its life in water comes onto land to bury up to several dozen eggs in a shallow hole it digs in late spring or early summer. Most turtle eggs hatch from August to October, with a peak in September.

Eastern musk turtle, 3 to 5.5 in.

Spotted turtle, 3.5 to 5 in.

Wood turtle, 5 to 9 in.

Painted turtle, typically 4 to 10 in.

If there were an animal Olympics, frogs would certainly be competitors in the standing long jump. Some can leap more than 30 times their body length.

Lots of animals are specialists physically. They have a feature that gives them an advantage over other animals in finding food or defending themselves, and that's why their species has survived over the centuries. Frogs use their tremendous jumping ability both to escape predators and to pounce on a meal.

Frogs are amphibians, which means they spend part of their lives in water and part on land. They are also among the animals that undergo metamorphosis, which means a "change in form." As young tadpoles (also called polliwogs), they live in water and look like small fish with large rounded heads. They have gills, tails and no legs. But eventually they develop lungs and legs, they will lose their tails and, as frogs, they will be able to live on land.

There may be nearly 4,800 species of frogs worldwide. (This includes toads, which technically are a kind of frog.) Some 16 species of frogs can be found in New Jersey.

Most adult frogs have large hind legs for jumping, hind toes that are connected by webbing, no claws and tiny teeth (if they have any at all).

Some, such as the eastern spadefoot, are rare enough in the state that you will probably never come across one in your

Bullfrog, 3 to 8 in.

lifetime. But others, like bullfrogs and green frogs, are so common that you can't miss them. In spring or summer, walk down to the edge of any pond and you may see a green frog sitting very still on the bank or a bullfrog peering at you from the water, its two bulging eyes and a bit of its head breaking the pond's surface.

Spend any time around a pond and you'll also hear frogs calling, or chorusing, especially during breeding season, which usually peaks in the spring. Male frogs are the ones making all the noise. They call to attract females and to announce that a territory is theirs. A frog enhances its call by using a loose pouch of skin at its throat that it can fill with air. When it calls, the sound enters this air-filled chamber and reverberates, like an echo in a cave, becoming even more intense. A male frog might repeat its call thousands of times in one night.

Nearly all female frogs lay jellylike eggs in water, often thousands of eggs at a time, which eventually hatch to become tadpoles.

In winter, frogs become inactive, settling down into the mud at the bottom of ponds or taking refuge under piles of dead leaves or in underground tunnels on land. In the coldest weather, some even partially freeze but are still able to thaw out and resume their lives in the spring.

Most frogs eat insects, such as ants and flies, as well as worms and snails. However, the bullfrog, which is the largest

Frog or toad?

You can usually tell the two apart by the texture of their skins. Frogs tend to have smoother skin, and they spend a lot of time in and around water. Toads have rougher, warty skin and usually can be found on land.

Leopard frog, 2 to 5 in.

American toad, 2 to 4.5 in.

Green frog, 2 to 4 in.

native New Jersey frog, will eat fish, snakes, mice and even small birds or newly hatched turtles that venture too close.

In recent years, biologists have noticed a growing problem among amphibians. Many have deformities, such as missing or extra limbs. In addition, populations of frogs in some places in the world are declining dramatically. Researchers are not sure what the reason is for the troubling problem. A leading theory is that it may be due to a disease or pesticides.

Gray treefrog, 1.5 to 2 in.

Humans vs. animals

The peak performance of humans as of 2015 compared with the observed performance of animals in the wild

Marathon
(26 miles, 385 yards)
Human: 2 hr., 2 min., 57 sec.
Pronghorn antelope: About 45 min.

High jump
Human: 8 ft., .5 in.
Killer whale: 15 to 17 ft.

Speed on land
(100 meter dash)
Human: 9.58 sec.
Cheetah: About 3.2 sec.

Speed in water
(100 meter freestyle)
Human: 46.91 sec.
Sailfish: About 3.3 sec.

Long jump
Human: 29 ft., 4.3 in.
Snow leopard: About 50 ft.

Vernal pools

Wood frog, 1.5 to 3.5 in.

Eastern spadefoot toad 1.5 to 3 in.

On the first warm night that follows a heavy rain each spring, an amazing event occurs. Certain frogs and salamanders that are rarely seen at any other time of the year come out of hiding and begin moving through the woods in great numbers.

Crowds of frogs. Parades of salamanders.

They are migrating to pools of water left by melted snow on forest floors. They may cross roads, hike up hills and climb over rocks and fallen trees in their determination to reach these temporary patches of water, called vernal pools.

Because the water dries up in the heat of summer, these pools do not contain fish. That makes them ideal breeding ponds for these amphibians, since there will be no predatory fish in the water to eat their eggs or their developing young.

In New Jersey, where there may be up to 5,000 vernal pools, wood frogs and eastern spadefoot toads make this trek, as do spotted, marbled, blue-spotted, eastern tiger and Jefferson salamanders.

During March and April, you can locate some of these breeding pools by the sounds that come from them at night. Wood frogs will chorus, making a noise that resembles ducks quacking. Once these amphibians reach their vernal pool, which they may return to year after year, they must court, breed and lay their eggs in a short period of time.

They are active by day, but most of the activity is at night, especially among the salamanders. If you can locate a vernal pool in the spring, take a flashlight, shine it on the water after dark, and you might see dozens of these creatures swimming about.

Spotted salamander 6 to 10 in.

What monarch butterflies do each fall is just about the definition of impossible.

Each September, tens of millions of these regal orange and black butterflies leave their summer breeding grounds in the United States and Canada and flutter off toward their winter home on a few remote mountainsides in Central Mexico. They return to the very same trees that previous generations returned to in their southern migrations for perhaps thousands of years. Then, in March, they may lift off nearly all at once, forming great clouds of butterflies that fill the sky as they return north.

A monarch butterfly rests in a field during migration

But the astounding thing is that adult monarchs may live less than one month in summer. That means that none of the monarchs that leave Mexico in the spring are among those that return in the fall. Instead, it is often their great-great-grandchildren that will somehow find their way back to those few Mexican mountainsides with no one in their band of migrating monarchs ever having been there.

How do they do it? Is it in their genes? Are they guided by the Earth's magnetic field? Or is it just one of the mysteries of animal instincts?

Butterflies, like most insects, go through a metamorphosis, or a change in appearance, except that for butterflies it is one of the most striking changes. Butterflies have four stages to their lives – egg, larva (also called a caterpillar), pupa (also called a chrysalis), then adult butterfly.

In the pupa stage, the caterpillar forms a shell-like covering around itself and hangs by thin threads from a twig or leaf. Inside, the caterpillar can change from a fairly clumsy, slow-moving and perhaps, to some, even ugly creature into what can be a beautiful, brilliantly colored butterfly, carrying the colors of a rainbow on its fragile wings.

Butterflies feed on nectar, a sweet liquid produced deep inside flowers. To do this, a butterfly uses its proboscis, a long narrow tube like a drinking straw that can be almost as long as its body. When it's not in use, the proboscis is kept curled up where you would expect the butterfly's mouth to be.

Butterflies need the heat of the sun to warm their bodies, so they tend to be most active during the middle of the day. At night, they rest.

Butterflies have three body parts – the head, the thorax or middle section, and the abdomen. They have six legs, and four wings – a pair each of front and back wings.

The colors on their wings are created by tiny colored scales that fit together like tiles in a mosaic.

Most adult butterflies live only two to four weeks, surviving long enough to mate and produce eggs. The female searches for certain kinds of plants on which to lay her eggs, since they are food plants for the young caterpillars. Monarchs choose milkweed. White admirals like wild cherry and poplar leaves. Tiger swallowtails prefer black cherry leaves.

There are about 125 species of butterflies that are seen through the year in New Jersey. Most breed in the state but some just stray into the state or are carried here by large storms or on strong winds from other states or regions of the country.

Butterfly or moth?

There are lots of differences. Butterflies usually fly during the day. Moths usually fly at night.

Butterflies tend to rest with their wings folded up over their heads or stretched flat to each side. Moths often lay their wings flat and behind them while resting.

The antennae of butterflies are thin and end in a knob. Those of moths do not end in a knob and are often feathery. Butterflies usually have bolder and brighter colors than moths, although there are some strikingly colored moths.

Moth

Butterfly

Baltimore checkerspot

Eastern black swallowtail

The science of butterfly wings

Butterflies are the supermodels of the insect kingdom, garbed in spectacular colors and sensational designs.

However, all that artistry has more purpose than to please the human eye. The hues, patterns and other features carried on those fragile wings have multiple purposes, all of them critical to survival – discouraging predators, generating heat and wooing the opposite sex.

For instance, some butterflies have evolved to have a feature on their wings called eyespots, which help to discourage predators. The little wood satyr has a pair of eyespots on the edges of both its front and back wings. They are spots that may appear to a poor-sighted predator to look like eyes. They can startle a predator like a bird or snake, buying the butterfly an instant of time in which to make its escape.

Swallowtail butterflies have small projections at the ends of their wings that look like tails (thus their name). These features evolved to attract the attention of predators who may attack the false tails, which tear off easily, giving the butterfly a chance to escape.

Butterflies, like snakes, frogs and turtles, don't have a way to create heat inside their body, the way humans do. They are the temperature of their surroundings and often have to warm up by basking in the sun.

People know that if they wear dark colors on a sunny day, they are likely to be warmer than if they wear light colors. Dark colors, such as brown and black, absorb more sunlight than light colors, such as yellow or white, and the absorbed sunlight creates heat.

The tail of the eastern tiger swallowtail, which tears away easily, can be a misleading target for predators.

The dark coloring of a mourning cloak absorbs sunlight, which creates heat in cold weather.

The eyespots of a little wood satyr may fool predators into attacking the outer wing edges instead of the head.

For butterflies, which need a way to generate heat on a cool day, this trait is important. Nearest to their bodies, most butterflies have dark colors. That's because butterflies need a body temperature of at least 80 degrees to fly well. Their muscles won't work properly otherwise. For this reason, butterflies that fly in the early spring or late fall or that overwinter as adults in the state, such as mourning cloaks, tend to have darker coloring.

However, the need for dark colors farther out on the wings isn't as great as it is near the body. That's because very little blood circulates in the wings and they are only able to transfer heat for a short distance.

Reproduction does require bright colors and distinctive patterns somewhere on a butterfly, not only to attract the eye of the opposite sex, but also to identify it as being of the same species. Females choose males based on how nicely and brightly colored they are. Males make the same kind of choices.

Once you know all this, an eastern tiger swallowtail's features makes a lot more sense: dark near its body for heat, false tails on its wings to foil predators, and fantastic yellow coloring with black patterns on most of its wings to lure a mate.

The design of butterflies, besides being functional, is quite ancient. Human beings have only been around about two million years, but physically and intellectually we are a species that has changed dramatically. Butterflies, on the other hand, have been flitting from flower to flower and sporting colorful patterns on their wings for more than 40 million years, with few evolutionary alterations. That must mean their design has worked well for them.

CHECKLIST
Common butterflies

Mourning cloak
3 – 3.5 in. wingspan
☐

Monarch
3.5 – 4 in.
☐

Eastern tiger swallowtail
3 – 5.5 in.
☐

Spicebush swallowtail
3.5 – 4.5 in.
☐

Eastern black swallowtail
2.5 – 3.5 in.
☐

Red-spotted purple
3 – 4 in.
☐

Red admiral
2 – 2.5 in.
☐

Great spangled fritillary
2 – 3 in.
☐

Baltimore checkerspot
1.5 – 2.5 in.
☐

Pearl crescent
1 – 1.5 in.
☐

Eastern comma
1.5 – 2 in.
☐

American copper
About 1 in.
☐

Painted lady
2 – 2.5 in.
☐

Spring azure
About 1 in.
☐

Cabbage white
1.5 – 2 in.
☐

Clouded sulphur
1.5 – 2 in.
☐

Silver-spotted skipper
1.5 – 2.5 in.
☐

Common ringlet
1 – 2 in.
☐

Little wood satyr
1.5 – 2 in.
☐

Banded hairstreak
1 – 1.5 in.
☐

Approximate flight times for New Jersey butterflies

(▬▬▬ = first generation, ▬▬▬ = second generation, ▬▬▬ = third generation)

	MAR	APR.	MAY	JUNE	JULY	AUG.	SEP.	OCT.	NOV.

Mourning cloak — Overwinters as an adult

Eastern comma — Overwinters as an adult

Cabbage white

Spring azure — Several overlapping broods through the summer

Tiger swallowtail

Clouded sulphur — Several overlapping broods through the summer

Red admiral — Two or three broods through the season

Painted lady

Spicebush swallowtail

American copper

Pearl crescent

Eastern black swallowtail

Little wood satyr

Common ringlet

Silver-spotted skipper — Two or three broods through the season

Red-spotted purple

Monarch — Three generations are mixed through the season. The last generation migrates to Mexico.

Baltimore checkerspot

Banded hairstreak

Great spangled fritillary

At most family reunions, get all the relatives together in one room and you can usually see a resemblance.

But put a caterpillar and a butterfly side by side, or a tadpole and a frog next to each other, and not only is there no family resemblance, there's not even a species resemblance. Why does this happen?

This dramatic change in appearance, this metamorphosis, evolved in nature as a way of ensuring that these species would survive.

Many features of plants and animals – the long legs of a great blue heron, the rich color of a rose, the sharp beak of a hawk – evolved or developed because they give a species a better chance for survival. They are features that give it an edge in finding food or in reproducing or in protecting itself from predators.

Metamorphosis is no different. Species that change form (and all amphibians and nearly all insects go through some type of metamorphosis) can occupy two very different places in the ecosystem. The young may eat one kind of food, go through metamorphosis, and then eat a different kind of food as adults. That means there is more food available for the entire species, increasing its chance for survival.

Tadpoles are vegetarians, but adult bullfrogs eat almost anything, from plants to flying insects. Most caterpillars feed on leaves, but adult butterflies sip the rich nectar they find in flowers.

Having different forms at different stages of life can help in other ways as well. Caterpillars do almost nothing but eat and grow, and they are well-designed to do just that. They are able to avoid predators to some extent because most can blend into vegetation. They are also able to blend into their environment as pupae, the stage in which they are surrounded by mummylike coverings and

A monarch pupa about to open

Monarch caterpillar

undergo the changes that make them adult butterflies. Then, in the butterfly stage, they can fly to new areas to lay eggs and spread their species.

The changes tadpoles and caterpillars go through during metamorphosis are striking. Bullfrog tadpoles, which will be going from a life spent entirely in water to a life on land and in water, have to develop limbs and lungs during the change, and their tails have to be reabsorbed into their bodies.

Caterpillars, during the pupa stage, have to lose their many legs as well as develop wings and sex organs. They will also develop new mouth parts to draw nectar from flowers as adult butterflies.

For frogs, the metamorphosis usually lasts from several days to a few weeks. For butterflies, it may last from a few days to several months.

Monarch metamorphosis

In about 10 days, the adult butterfly emerges from the pupa, unfolds its wings, which slowly harden, then it flies away.

In the pupa stage, wings develop and the mouth parts change from chewing parts to sucking parts so that the adult butterfly can sip flower nectar.

Eggs are laid by female monarchs on the undersides of the leaves of milkweed plants. Each larva, or caterpillar, will eat its way out of its egg within a week and then begin to feed on the milkweed.

For the next two to three weeks, the caterpillar will feed and grow, shedding its skin every so often, a process called molting.

The caterpillar attaches itself by a silk thread and tiny hooks on its abdomen to a plant stalk and then sheds its skin one last time to reveal the pupa beneath.

Bullfrog metamorphosis

Within an egg, the embryonic cell divides within the first half day, and at four days, the developing tadpole has a tail bud and some muscle movement.

During reproduction, the male clasps the female, and she lays thousands of eggs in water. He then fertilizes the eggs with his sperm.

The egg hatches in water in about six days, and the tadpole clings to plants underwater. Within a day, it will begin to feed on algae.

A bullfrog spends about two years as a tadpole.

When the metamorphosis starts, hind legs begin to appear, and the gill system is gradually replaced by a lung system.

The frog is a mature adult in about three years. Adult bullfrogs typically weigh about one pound.

Within two weeks, the metamorphosis is usually complete. With its lungs, a frog can breathe air.

Ruby meadowhawk, female

As if the passion of the public for boldly colored winged creatures can't be satisfied by birds and butterflies alone, dragonflies are now attracting their faithful followers.

And why not? They are elegant creatures, capable of mid-air acrobatics that few, if any, birds can match. They are also the friends of anyone who doesn't like mosquitoes. The reason dragonflies spend so much time hovering over ponds is that they are hunting mosquitoes, which are their primary food.

Worldwide, there are about 6,000 species in the order Odonata, which includes dragonflies and damselflies. Nearly 180 can be found in New Jersey – 52 or so species of damselflies and 127 or so of dragonflies.

Like birds, dragonflies fly and lay eggs. Some, like the green darner, even migrate to warmer regions when the weather turns cold. However, like butterflies and other insects, dragonflies undergo metamorphosis, changing from waterbound larvae to flying adults. Unlike butterflies, though, there is no pupa stage.

The eggs of dragonflies, which are laid in or near water, hatch in five to 10 days. The larvae that emerge then begin the process of eating and growing. They consume everything from mosquito larvae to tiny fish, capturing their prey with a unique lower lip that has its own

Twelve-spotted skimmer, male

claw. The lip can shoot out to almost a third of a larva's body length to grab a meal.

Larvae that hatch in the summer often spend the winter growing before transforming into adult dragonflies the following spring.

When it is ready to make the change to a flying adult, the larva climbs out of the water, takes hold of a reed or twig, and sheds its skin, allowing the soft, folded wings beneath to slowly fill with blood and harden. Within an hour or two, the adult dragonfly takes to the air.

Many dragonflies live only about a month as adults, time enough to mate (usually accomplished in mid-air) and to lay eggs before dying.

The flight abilities of dragonflies are indeed impressive. The larger species, such as the darners, may be capable of flying up to 50 miles per hour. Seemingly tireless, they may spend most of the day in the air, catching prey on the wing.

What makes them such powerful aviators? For one thing, like a hummingbird, a high percentage of their body mass is dedicated to flight. A sexually mature male may be more than 60 percent flight muscle.

Dragonflies can take off backward, they can launch vertically like a helicopter, and they can hover motionless for more than a minute. They can also stop on a dime.

Dragonfly or damselfly?

Dragonflies and damselflies are both found flying over ponds, swamps and other still water bodies. You can tell the two apart by how they hold their wings when at rest. A dragonfly will stretch them out from side to side. Damselflies, which have thin, needle-like bodies, rest with their wings folded in back of them close to their sides. Contrary to myth, neither dragonflies nor damselflies bite humans.

Dragonfly

Damselfly

Halloween
pennant,
male

Dragonflies mating

Bluet, male, a damselfly

Green darner,
female

American lady

Monarch

Eastern tiger swallowtail

What tangled webs they weave. Worldwide, nearly 44,000 kinds of spiders have been identified, including about 3,000 in the United States and nearly 600 species in New Jersey.

You can tell a spider by its two body sections and eight legs. (Since insects have only six legs, spiders are not true insects.)

Interestingly, most spiders also have eight eyes, with some found on the side instead of the front of their bodies. Yet, spiders have poor eyesight generally.

Many spiders are active only at night, and most are not very aggressive. Even those with the strongest venom will attack humans only as a defensive measure, preferring to retreat from battle whenever possible.

Because of the Northeast's chilly winters, most spiders found in New Jersey live just one season, hatching in the spring, breeding and laying eggs in the summer, and dying in the fall. But a certain number manage to live through the winter. They may try to escape harsh weather by seeking refuge in the cozy interior of your home or apartment. A large house can be home to hundreds of spiders in winter, with the human residents barely aware of their presence.

Most spiders you are likely to encounter in New Jersey would be too small to pose a threat. As a general rule, only those with a body over half an inch in length (not including legs) have fangs capable of penetrating human skin. But that does not mean they are dangerous. Even larger spiders that bite are not usually a serious danger.

Just about all spiders are venomous. Even the smaller ones use venom to weaken or kill their prey. But only a

The multiple eyes of a spider

few spiders have strong enough venom to cause harm to a human being.

The two most venomous spiders to be found in the United States are the brown recluse and the black widow. However, most people recover if bitten by either.

The black widow is native to New Jersey, however the brown recluse is not. It is usually found in the south-central United States but can arrive here as a stowaways on food, furniture or clothes brought into the area from those states where it is a native.

Among the largest spiders you might cross paths with in New Jersey are these two, shown their actual size. They can be found in homes or sheds near forested areas. Their venom is not poisonous to humans.

Brownish-gray fishing spider, female, 1 in.

Wolf spider, female, 1 in.

Nursery web spider, female, .6 in.

The brown recluse has a violin-shaped mark on its back. Its bite can have serious effects and must be treated quickly.

The female black widow is black with a red marking on her abdomen that is shaped like an hourglass. The female earned her name because soon after mating she may eat the male. The males of most species of spiders are not treated so badly.

Crab spider, female, .4 in.

One of the largest spiders someone in New Jersey` might encounter indoors is the wolf spider, often a resident of garden sheds and suburban gardens. However, sometimes it is an invader of homes. Its body can be more than an inch long. While painful, its bite usually does not have long-lasting effects. In most species, the female is larger than the male.

Southern black widow spider, female, .5 in.

Brown recluse spider, female, .4 in.

Spider webs

The delicate webs that decorate dew-covered meadows or that float weightlessly in the corners of attic ceilings are actually wonders of engineering. Pound for pound, the silk in a spider web is stronger than steel.

Spiders produce the silk in their abdomens. It starts out as a sticky gel made of pure protein that is created in an array of glands. The gel is pushed down tubes that lead to ducts called spinnerets that will shoot it out of the body.

By contracting its abdomen muscles, a spider is able to push out the gel from thousands of tiny spigots on the spinnerets. In the process, the gel changes to a solid. And like the many fibers that come together to create hemp rope, so the many strands exiting the spigots come together to create the finished silk line.

The final strand of silk may be less than a tenth the thickness of a human hair, but it can hold an astounding amount of weight.

As a comparison, a rope that is an inch thick would have to support as many as 15 automobiles to have the same strength as some spider silk.

Aside from creating webs with their silk to snare passing flies and other prey, spiders use it as a safety line so that they can drop down from ceilings or branches. They also use silk to wrap their eggs for protection and to wrap prey for a later meal. A spider may produce up to eight kinds of silk, each for a different use.

Watch a colony of ants around their nest in a field or a swarm of gnats on a pond in summer and almost inevitably the question occurs to you.

Just how many insects are there in the world?

Well, science has an answer – or at least a rough estimate. At any given moment on the planet, there are about 10 quintillion of them. That's roughly 10,000,000,000,000,000,000 mayflies, millipedes, monarchs, mantises and more.

An impressive number, it's the best guess of famed Harvard entomologist E. O. Wilson. To put it in perspective, 10 quintillion is more than the number of seconds that would have ticked on a clock if it began keeping time the moment the universe began.

Worldwide, nearly a million species of insects have been identified. That's more than the number of all other species of animals combined. (There may be nearly 5,500 species of mammals and about 10,000 species of birds.) However, scientists say they have recorded only a fraction of all the insect species that actually exist, which they say may number more than two million.

Insects are found in just about every environment on Earth, including in Antarctica where several dozen species of insects have been seen.

If for no other reason than their sheer numbers, insects are arguably

Bumblebee, .7 in.

Honey bee, .5 in.

the most successful animals on the planet. Sure, they can be some of the most repellent creatures known to humankind, but they are perhaps more necessary to our survival than any other group of animals. They play a critical role in the ecology of Earth in ways that most people don't realize. Should insects all disappear at once, humans would soon follow since the lives of insects and humans are so intertwined.

Why? Insects are eaten by small animals, which are in turn eaten by bigger animals, which might ultimately be eaten by humans, so the entire food chain would fall apart. Also, insects pollinate the majority of fruits and vegetables humans eat, including apples, oranges, blueberries, cranberries, cherries, melons and almonds. Insects also break down dead plants and animals as well as animal wastes into the nutrients that fertilize the soil, allowing things to grow.

Then, there is the less measurable spiritual loss the disappearance of beetles and butterflies, ladybugs and waterbugs, would create. Most flowering plants, including field wildflowers, are pollinated by insects, so they would also disappear. Indeed, some of the poetry would go out of our daily lives.

Insects are the ultimate survivors, despite their small size and short lives. (Some adult mosquitoes are lucky to live two weeks). In fact, their brief lives

Bee or wasp?

Both can sting if bothered. Bees tend to have hairy bodies while wasps usually do not. Many bees, such as bumblebees and honey bees, have on their hind legs "pollen baskets" made of stiff hairs, where they carry the pollen they collect on their visits to flowers. Wasps do not have them. Hornets and yellow jackets are kinds of wasps.

Bumblebee

Paper wasp

Woolly bear caterpillar, 2 in.

Praying mantis, 3.5 in.

True katydid, 2 in.

help make them so successful in surviving change. Insects reproduce quickly and in great numbers. So if there is any change in their surroundings – for instance, if the temperature warms dramatically – the chances are good that they will produce some young from the thousands of eggs they might lay (some termite queens produce 30,000 eggs a day) that have the right combination of genes to overcome the warmer weather. Some of those young will survive, reproduce more young with similar genes, and soon the local population will have adapted to the warmer climate and be thriving again.

Pennsylvania leather-wing

Species that take a relatively long time to reproduce, such as some birds, which may have just two or three young a season, would not be able to adapt to dramatic changes in their habitat so quickly. Such changes might completely wipe out their local population.

All insects have certain things in common. They have six legs, three body sections and antennae. Spiders, with their eight legs, are not true insects. Most insects can hear, taste, touch, smell and see, but many of them do these things in very different ways than humans. Crickets hear with their knees. Flies taste with their feet. Some moths and beetles smell with their antennae.

Most insects have two main eyes and two or three smaller, simpler eyes. The main eyes are sometimes made up of thousands of individual lenses, each of which produces an image. Human eyes have one lens each, so the human brain has to interpret only the two images that its eyes send it. But a dragonfly's eyes may have 28,000 lenses each, which means its tiny brain has to interpret that many separate signals in order to understand what it is seeing.

Nearly every insect goes through metamorphosis, a change in appearance marking a new stage of its life. Most insects look different as adults than as young emerging from eggs. Many are flightless when young but have wings as adults.

Big bugs

Here are a few of the larger insects that can be found in New Jersey. They are shown their actual sizes.

Fiery searcher

Eastern dobsonfly

Dogday harvestfly (cicada)

Luna moth

Fireflies

Also called lightning bugs, these beetles produce light in the tips of their abdomens by combining chemicals they produce and store in their bodies. Their blinking in summer is part of their mating process. Males fly about, flashing their lights to attract females that sit on leaves and branches.

There are nearly 200 species of fireflies in North America. A few don't flash, but those that do have their own pattern of flashes to help males and females of the same species identify each other.

In the East, the male of one of the most common fireflies (*Photinus pyralis*) flashes in low flight over grass about every six seconds, creating a yellowish "J" that lasts about half a second as he lifts into the air. The female, which sits on vegetation nearby, responds about two seconds later with a half-second flash of her own, an invitation for him to approach.

Ants

Like bees and other social insects, ants live in organized societies in which the members work together to keep the colony functioning. In all ant colonies, one queen ant is responsible for laying the eggs and producing the young.

Black carpenter ants, which are about a half-inch long, build their nests in dead wood, creating a series of tunnels and rooms. Unlike termites, they do not eat wood. They only tunnel into it.

Little black ants, which may be one-fourth the size of carpenter ants, usually build their nest underground, forming a little mound at the opening.

Mosquitoes

It is only the female mosquito that will bite you. The males feed mainly on flower nectar and fruit juices. The females need a meal of blood before laying eggs. Mosquitoes are most active at dawn, at dusk and at night. They hatch from eggs that develop in water, such as rainwater that collects in roadside ditches or in discarded tires.

Grasshoppers and crickets

The "songs" of grasshoppers, like those of crickets, are the music of summer nights. However, these insects don't sing the way humans do. Grasshoppers rub a rough part of a back leg against their wings to create their music, and crickets rub their wings together. They make these noises to attract females and to chase away other males.

Ladybugs

Probably the best known of beetles, ladybugs are among the most valuable beetles to humans. They generally do not eat plants, but they do eat small insects that eat plants, which makes them important to farmers. In this region, you might see ladybugs with as few as zero spots or with as many as 19.

June bugs

Also called May beetles, June bugs are often seen buzzing around porch lights, or they are heard crashing into windows and screens at night.

Unfortunately for them, they are attracted to electric lights. They are harmless to humans, though. As adults, they feed on the leaves of many common trees.

House flies

Unwelcome guests at a picnic and a noisy distraction when they get inside a home or apartment, house flies live short lives and reproduce quickly. But they do not bite.

Their eggs can hatch in just a day, and the larvae can grow to adulthood in a week. A house fly may be hatched, mature, reproduce and die in the space of just a month, which means several generations of house flies can emerge during one summer.

Honey bees

Honey bees live in ordered communities in which each bee has a job. A honey bee hive may have 50,000 members. There is only one queen bee, and her job is to lay eggs. There may be 1,000 male drones in the hive, and their only job is to mate with the queen, although only one will be successful. The rest of the hive's members are female worker bees, and they can have many jobs during their brief lives. Here is the typical life cycle of one worker bee in summer.

DAY 1–3
The egg is laid and develops within a wax cell.

DAY 4–20
The larva emerges from the egg, feeds, and then develops into an adult worker bee.

DAY 21–23
The worker bee's first job is as a cleaner, readying the brood cells for the next batch of eggs.

DAY 24–27
It becomes a nurse, feeding the older larvae.

DAY 28–34
It continues as a nurse, feeding the younger larvae and the queen.

DAY 35–41
It becomes a food collector, searching outside the hive for pollen, a rich source of protein.

DAY 42–death
It continues as a food collector, searching outside the hive for nectar, a rich source of energy.

At different times, the worker bee may also be a fanner (beating its wings to keep the hive cool), an undertaker (removing the bodies of dead bees from the hive), a soldier (guarding the hive's entrance) or a builder (creating wax to add to the hive walls).

Japanese beetle

Cecropia caterpillars

Periodical cicada

Asian ladybug

Red-legged grasshopper

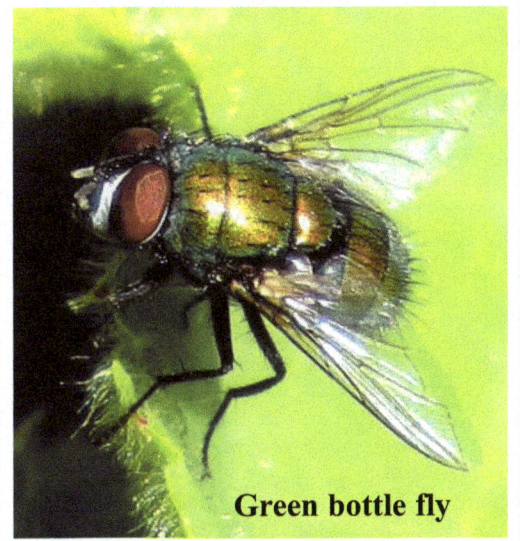

Green bottle fly

Same planet, different worlds.

That's a good definition of ecosystems, the largely self-contained collections of plants, animals and ecological conditions that cover the landscape like different countries on a map.

A pond with bullfrogs, cattails and dragonflies can be near a forest where you might see hemlocks, wolf spiders and white-tailed deer. And just a stone's throw away can be a field where you might find monarch butterflies, oxeye daisies and meadow voles.

An ecosystem is a collection of living and non-living things, including plants, animals, ponds, streams, rocks and dirt, that all interact as a unit.

An ecosystem is created by a particular combination of water, land features, sunlight and temperature. Wherever you find that set of physical conditions in a region, you're likely to find the same general group of plants and animals.

An ecosystem can include a stream or a pond, or it can include a combination of a stream and a pond. An ecosystem can include a meadow in a valley or a meadow on a mountainside.

An ecosystem can be as small as a single small pool of water left from melted snow on a forest floor in spring, or it can be as large as the whole forest, including the pool of water. Ecosystems are also found in cities. A vacant lot between two buildings may eventually become home to a variety of wildflowers, insects, birds and small mammals.

Ecosystems do not have barriers between them, though. They overlap and share resources. Insects, birds and other animals move between ecosystems.

Food web

In any ecosystem, relationships develop between plants and animals in regard to food, and those relationships are called a food web. In a forest ecosystem where oak trees grow, acorns and other nuts are an important element of the food web. Here is just a part of the food web in such a forest. The arrows indicate what feeds on what.

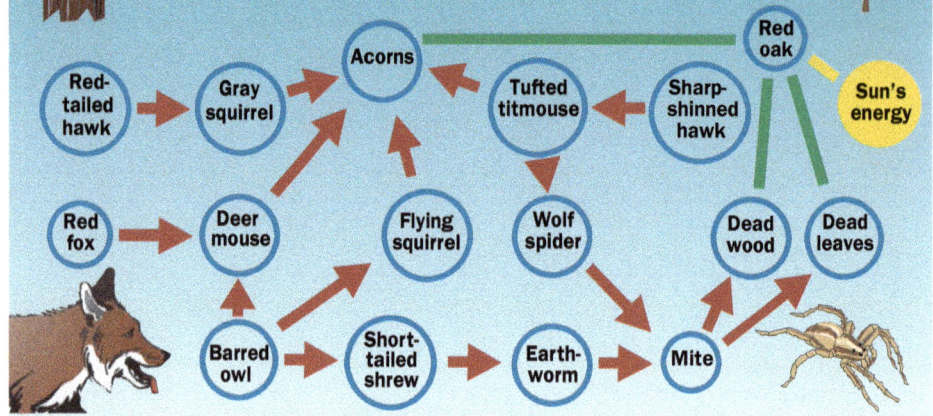

In nature, plants and animals depend on each other for food. Many birds eat insects. Many insects eat the leaves of trees and other plants. Trees and other plants draw nutrition through their roots from dead plants and animals that decay on the ground, and they produce nuts and seeds that birds and other animals eat. This is called a food web.

After a long period of time, a balance or a harmony in the food web in an ecosystem is often reached so that populations of the different species stay within certain limits. For instance, if a predator, such as foxes, grows too plentiful, the prey, such as deer mice, might die off. Without enough food, foxes might decline in number and the mice have a chance to grow more plentiful again, allowing foxes to grow in population once again. It is a continuing cycle.

Ecozones of New Jersey

In an ecozone, the same general physical conditions tend to prevail. Here are some of the characteristics of the region's different ecozones.

1   North central Appalachians
Mostly forested elevated plateau – High hills and low mountains – Sandstone, shale, siltstone, conglomerate, some coal

2   Ridge and valley
Roughly parallel ridges and valleys of various elevations – About 50% forested – Limestone, dolomite, shale, siltsone, sandstone

3   Northeastern highlands
Sparsely populated with poor soils – low mountains in southwest and central portion, and high hills in the northeast – Northern hardwood and spruce fir forests

4   Northeastern coastal zone
Many glacial lakes and poor soils – Forests and residential development in fairly flat coastal region – Densely populated

5   Northern Piedmont
Low rounded hills, irregular plains and open valleys – Appalachian oak forests – Sandstone, shale, conglomerate, siltstone

6   Atlantic coastal pine barrens
Sandy poor soils with stunted oaks and pines – Relatively flat with a few hills of erosion resistant bedrock, but generally under 100 feet

7   Mid-Atlantic coastal plain
A flat plain with many swamps and marshes – Forests of pine, oak, gum and cypress – More cropland in the north than in the south where soils are poorly drained

Examples of New Jersey ecosystems

Cattail marsh

Often found where soil is semi-permanently flooded and the standing water is shallow, these marshes are dominated by common cattails. The marshes are often beside open water, such as a lake. Red-winged blackbirds may nest among the cattails, and beavers may build lodges nearby. Snapping turtles, water snakes and various frogs, including bullfrogs and green frogs, live here. Skunk cabbage may bloom in the early spring in the shallows or on adjacent land.

Successional old field

When farm land or cleared fields are allowed to grow free, grasses and wildflowers are typically the first plants to take root, followed by smaller shrubs and trees and then finally larger trees that may shade out and eliminate the original undergrowth. Wildflowers found here include New England asters, dandelions and Queen Anne's lace. Animals seen here include eastern cottontails, meadow voles, field sparrows, red foxes, woodchucks and white-tailed deer. Successional old fields occur statewide.

Northern hardwood forest

The top of these forests – the canopy – is typically closed by leaves, providing shade beneath. Trees found here include sugar maples, yellow birches and American beeches. Mammals found here include white-tailed deer, black bears, porcupines, eastern chipmunks and red squirrels. Birds found here include black-capped chickadees and blue jays. Because of the shading by trees, many wildflowers, such as wood anemones, bloom in the early spring before leaves appear.

Floodplain forest

These are forests found along almost any river or large stream that floods regularly. The tree species found in them typically include silver and black maple, cottonwood, butternut, sycamore, black willow and ash. Plants seen here include jewelweed, Virginia creeper and poison ivy. Birds include red-bellied woodpeckers, cerulean warblers and tufted titmice. Great blue herons may nest in these forests. Amphibians include Jefferson salamanders and leopard frogs.

Urban vacant lot

Vacant lots in towns and cities can become home to a range of wildlife. Trees found here include tree-of-heaven, white mulberry and Norway maples. Wildflowers found here include Queen Anne's lace, dock and goldenrod. Birds found here include starlings, house sparrows and pigeons. Mice and chipmunks may also be seen here, and cats may prowl at night, looking for a meal.

Coastal sand dune

This is a strip of shifting sands on which sparse vegetation and stunted trees, such as pitch pine, often grow. Erosion of the dunes by wind and storm-driven waves is common. Rugosa rose, beach heath and poison ivy are common plants as are various grasses that hold the dune in place. Birds, such as the piping plover, and sea turtles, such as the diamondback terrapin, nest here.

Rock outcrop

These are areas typically on upper mountain slopes where bedrock is visible and there are only pockets of thin soil. As a result, trees tend to be stunted and other plants can be sparse. Peregrine falcons may nest here and timber rattlesnakes may den here. Mosses and lichens may cover the rocks, but the wildlife found here will depend on the kind of bedrock and its elevation.

Water lily aquatic wetland

Found throughout the state, these ecosystems are often associated with ponds, lakes and slow-moving sections of rivers. Plant species seen here include fragrant water lily and spatterdock. Green frogs, bullfrogs and dragonflies are common, and birds seen here may include great blue herons and mallards.

Appalachian oak forest

This is a forest mainly of hardwood trees that is usually found on ridgetops and slopes. Trees found here include red and white oaks, red maples and hickories. Oaks produce acorns, so animals seen here include those that feed on acorns, such as gray squirrels, deer mice and wild turkeys. Birds seen here include hawks that feed on small mammals, as well as blue jays and tufted titmice. Timber rattlesnakes may also be found here.

Bluegill – 4 to 12 in., typical
length for adults –
fresh water

White perch – 8 to 10 in. –
fresh and salt water

Smallmouth bass –
8 to 15 in. – fresh water

Rainbow trout – 10 to 25 in. – fresh
and salt water

Striped bass – 18 to 45 in. –
fresh and salt water

This planet was made for fish. Nearly 71 percent of the Earth's surface is covered by the oceans. Add in the countless lakes, ponds, rivers and streams on land and it's clear that uncounted billions of fish call all this water home.

New Jersey has nearly 18,000 miles of rivers and streams flowing through it. The state also has more than 4,000 lakes, ponds and reservoirs over an acre in size. And about 135 species of freshwater fish can be found in these inland waters. The state also has 130 miles of coastline along the Atlantic Ocean and thousands more species call the Atlantic home.

Some fish, such as the yellow perch and bluegill, are found only in freshwater habitats. You will find the halibut and great white shark only in the salt water of the ocean. However, the striped killifish and the mummichog spend most of their time in the mixed waters of estuaries, such as Delaware Bay, Raritan Bay and Great Bay.

Some fish split their time between fresh water and salt water. American shad spend most of their time out at sea in salt water, then they come up rivers, including the Delaware River, to spawn (reproduce) in the spring in freshwater environments. The American eel does just the opposite, laying its eggs in salt water but living mostly in fresh water.

Fish evolved well before land animals, first appearing nearly 500 million years ago. Most scientists believe land animals can claim fish as their ancestors. They believe amphibians, such as salamanders and frogs, evolved directly from fish; reptiles, such as snakes and turtles, evolved from amphibians; and birds and mammals, including human beings, evolved separately from reptiles.

Fish breathe underwater by drawing oxygen from water as it passes over their gills. Sharks are fish, but whales (including dolphins and porpoises, which are kinds of whales) are mammals and they breathe air into their lungs like human beings, holding their breath when they submerge. Some whales can stay submerged for more than an hour on one breath.

Most fish are among those animals whose reproductive strategy is to lay lots of eggs and then abandon them. Enough eggs usually develop that their species will survive. Fish usually produce thousands or even millions of eggs each season. A female bluefin tuna may produce 10 million eggs in a single year.

Some sharks lay eggs, but others give birth to live young that hatch from eggs inside the mother and then eat other eggs or developing young before being born.

Trophy fish

Here are the record weights, in pounds and ounces, as of April, 2015, for some species of fish caught in New Jersey inland and coastal waters.

Yellow perch – 2 lb. 6 oz
Bluegill – 3 lb.
Smallmouth bass – 7 lb. 2 oz.
Chain pickerel – 9 lb. 3 oz.
Largemouth bass – 10 lb. 14 oz.
American shad – 11 lb. 1 oz.
Rainbow trout – 13 lb. 0 oz.
Bluefish – 27 lb. 1 oz.
Northern Pike – 30 lb. 8.5 oz.
Lake trout – 32 lb. ç
Channel catfish – 33 lb. 3 oz.
Carp – 47 lb.
Striped bass – 78 lb. 8 oz,√
Cod – 81 lb.
Swordfish – 530 lb.
Tiger shark – 880 lb.
Bluefin tuna – 1,030 lb. 6 oz.
Blue marlin – 1,046 lb.

An osprey with a spotted seatrout

The oceans were home to living things well before the land was. And just as land animals have evolved to take forms that increase their species' chance of survival, so have marine creatures.

Finding food and trying not to be something else's food are two of the main reasons why different forms of life have the different forms they do. To be fast on land so that you can escape predators or so that you can be a predator yourself, you need strong legs and a sleek runner's body, like an antelope or a cheetah. If you're not going to be a fast runner, you need something else that protects you, like the tough outer shell of a turtle. You can also be well protected if you have the huge size of an elephant or the small size of a spider, which can hide from predators in tiny openings.

Harbor seal

Common starfish

In the water, the same rules hold true. A marine creature survives best if it has speed or a protective physical feature.

To be fast swimmers, many marine animals, such as sharks and dolphins, have smooth, torpedo-shaped bodies so that they can cut easily through the water. Many of the slow movers, such as clams, lobsters and horseshoe crabs, have a hard outer shell. Summer flounders have camouflage. They are flat fish that lie on the

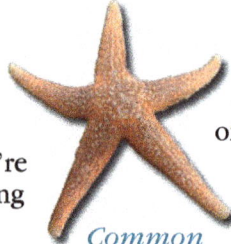
Horseshoe crab

ocean bottom, settling into the sand and changing their color to match their surroundings.

The huge size of whales makes them safe from most marine predators. And the fourspine stickleback - a very small fish, only about two inches in length - stays close to underwater vegetation near shorelines, where it can hide from larger predatory fish that come near.

Starfish have a unique way to increase their chances of survival. A predator may take a bite out of a starfish, but even if it loses four of its five arms and most of its central disk, a starfish can still regrow its entire body.

Laws also protect some ocean animals. Several decades ago, harbor and gray seals were rare sights in New Jersey waters. Some would occasionally take fish from fishermen's nets, so bounties were offered for dead seals. However, the federal Marine Mammal Protection Act was passed in 1972 and now thousands of seals are seen in winter on or near the state's beaches, from Sandy Hook to Cape May. However, seals attract great white sharks and seals can be a headache for fishermen and people who own beach property. So there are those who don't welcome them back.

Ghost crab

Seashell collection

The shells found on beaches were once the portable homes of living marine creatures.

Northern quahog

2.5 to 4 in. – Also called hard-shelled clams, quahogs usually live in protected bays and inlets.

Soft-shelled clam

1 to 5.5 in. – These shellfish, also known as steamer clams, are usually found in sand or mud.

Eastern oyster

2 to 8 in. – Oysters are usually found below the low-tide line. They are often found in clusters.

Channeled whelk

3 to 8 in. – Whelks are sea snails, and channeled whelks are found from Cape Cod to Florida on sandy or muddy ocean bottoms.

Blue mussel

1 to 4 in. – Mussels often form great colonies, attaching to rocks, shells, wood pilings or other solid structures near or below the low-tide mark.

Atlantic bay scallop

1.5 to 4 in. – These scallops normally live in the shallow water of protected bays where sea grasses grow.

Common periwinkle

1 in. or less – Periwinkles often attach to rocks or vegetation in the zone between low and high tide where they feed on algae.

Knobbed whelk

4 to 9 in. – These marine snails feed on clams. They are typically found in sand in shallow water.

Humpback whale

Humpback whale breaching

Whale hunters once sailed the ocean off Cape May. Now those same waters are the destination for the ships of whale watchers.

There are at least a half dozen species of whales, including humpbacks and finbacks, that have been seen off the New Jersey coast in the last few decades. That number increases if you include dolphins and porpoises, which, technically, are kinds of whales.

Whales are divided into two groups – baleen whales and toothed whales. Finback and humpback whales are baleen whales, which means they capture small fish by straining them out of water using features (baleens) that hang from their upper jaws and look like the teeth of a comb. The water can pass through, but fish do not.

Killer whales, sperm whales, dolphins and porpoises are toothed whales. They capture prey with their teeth and strong jaws. While fish are their primary food, killer whales may also hunt seals, dolphins, squid or even other whales.

The most common whale to be seen in New Jersey ocean waters is the humpback, a baleen whale. Humpbacks are slow swimmers, but they can be quite acrobatic, jumping out of the water at times, an action called breaching. For whale watchers, to see a whale breaching is a treasured sight.

It's estimated there are about 12,000 humpback whales remaining in the north Atlantic.

Only rarely seen in the north Atlantic is the blue whale. In 2010, a blue whale was detected migrating past New Jesey by researchers using equipment to listen for its distinctive call. The heaviest animal that has ever lived on earth, the blue whale can be more than 100 feet long and can weigh 300,000 pounds – more than 100 cars.

Whales are mammals and, like land-dwelling mammals, they give birth to live young, they have lungs and they breathe air.

Although some whales can remain underwater for more than an hour at a time, they all must come to the surface periodically to breathe. When a whale does surface, it forcefully exhales by shooting out a spout of air and water vapor from a "blowhole" on the top of its head. The spout from a blue whale may rise more than 30 feet.

It is a general rule in nature that the larger an animal is, the longer it tends to live. (Turtles, some of which can live a century, are one exception.) Whales can live long lives. Humpback whales may live 50 years, and some finbacks and right whales may live 90 years or more.

Dolphin or porpoise?

Dolphins, with their long snouts, are often more playful than porpoises and will usually venture closer to people and boats. Porpoises have shorter noses and tend to be shyer creatures than dolphins.

Whales of New Jersey coastal waters

Minke whale
20 to 30 ft. – These whales sometimes feed near coasts and may swim into bays and estuaries.

Atlantic white-sided dolphin
7 to 9 ft. – These dolphins, which are a type of whale, sometimes travel in large schools numbering as many as 1,000 individuals.

Humpback whale
40 to 50 ft. – Humpbacks, which can weigh 50 tons, are probably the favorite of whale watchers. When they breach and fall back into the water, the sound can be heard for miles.

Finback or fin whale
50 to 70 ft. – Second in size to blue whales, finbacks are streamlined and can swim up to 30 miles per hour. Despite their size, they are capable of leaping out of the water.

Right whale
35 to 50 ft. – There may be only 350 to 450 of these whales left in the world due to overhunting. Whalers called them the "right" whale to hunt because they were slow swimmers and floated when dead.

Right whale and calf

Gray seals

Common dolphins

Great black-backed gull with flounder

Blue whale

Harbor seal

Bottlenose dolphins

Great white shark

In weather not fit for man or beast, the beasts and other forms of wildlife manage to do a pretty good job of surviving in winter.

Through the ages, plants and animals have gained a variety of tricks for getting through even the most severe winter weather.

Some animals hibernate, sleeping through the worst of it. Others know how and where to avoid biting winds and freezing temperatures and where to find food in a pinch.

Birds can seem the most vulnerable of animals in winter, but they often ride out storms perched high up inside the layered branches of dense evergreen trees, sheltered from the snow and wind, sleeping or eating insects they find in the bark and under limbs. Their feathers offer natural protection from the cold. They can also fluff up their feathers with air for even greater insulation.

In winter, some birds will form great flocks, sometimes thousands of birds, and spend the night together in trees or other suitable locations, partially for warmth and partially for protection from predators and cold winter winds.

Around dusk each day, streams of crows can be seen flying toward their overnight site, called a roost. The location of the roost may move nightly. Particularly large roosts have occurred in Trenton, Bridgetown and Newark in some years.

Woodchucks and bats hibernate through the winter.

Raccoon

Red fox

Winter survival strategies

White pine

The needles of evergreens, such as pines, are not very sensitive to cold because of molecules within their cells that act like antifreeze in a car. Also, the cells contain low amounts of water.

Day lily

Some plants, like corn, die completely at the first frost, leaving their seeds behind to produce new plants in the spring. In others, like day lilies, the parts above ground die when winter arrives, but underground roots and stems live to grow again in the spring.

Sugar maple

Leaf-bearing trees, such as maples, shed their frost-sensitive leaves in the fall and move a lot of their water and nutrients – their sap – into their roots, away from cold temperatures.

Honey bee

Honey bees form large clusters inside their hives and create heat by shivering or beating their wings. To prevent the bees on the outside of the cluster from freezing to death, those on the inside change places with them from time to time.

Beavers spent the winter awake in their lodges. Rabbits take refuge in tunnels under snow-covered shrubs or in abandoned woodchuck holes. For these and other mammals, their fur is their winter coat.

For coyotes, red foxes, bobcats and a variety of birds of prey that choose not to migrate, such as red-tailed hawks, winter in this region is business as usual as they prowl and patrol the countryside for a meal. Snow can actually benefit them since it can make prey stand out.

For both plants and animals, the greatest danger of severe cold is that it can freeze water. When water does freeze, it expands and forms sharp-edged ice crystals. The cells of all living things are filled with water, and if that water turns to ice, it can puncture the cell walls, causing damage or even death.

Perhaps the most fantastic trick for surviving freezing

Snowy owl

temperatures is the one used by some frogs. Many frogs spend the winter on land, buried beneath leaves on the forest floor. But it may become so cold that even these places have freezing temperatures. To cope with such conditions, treefrogs, wood frogs and even spring peepers have found a way to turn to ice in winter, their bodies nearly frozen solid, and still survive. With just a few warm spring days, they will thaw out and begin to do the things frogs normally do in the spring.

How do they do it? They create chemical "seeds" within their body cavities but outside the cells of their organs and other body tissues. When the temperature drops below freezing, ice crystals will form around the seeds so that the water inside the cells does not freeze. Up to two-thirds of a frog's body water can freeze, yet it can remain alive because its cells are unharmed.

Hibernation

While many animals sleep through much of the winter, not all hibernate. True hibernation involves a dramatic decline in both the heart rate and the body temperature. For instance, the heart rate of a woodchuck falls from 100 beats per minute when active to 15 during hibernation, and its body temperature falls from 96 degrees to 47 degrees Fahrenheit. Snakes, turtles and frogs hibernate, but among mammals in New York, the true hibernators are the woodchuck, jumping mouse, chipmunk (although it will emerge from sleep to eat periodically) and several species of bats.

Black bears are not true hibernators. Their body temperature does not fall significantly. Skunks and raccoons will sleep through the winter but they do not hibernate. Birds that remain in the area during winter do not hibernate, but they do sleep. However, it is a different kind of sleep than the sleep of mammals. It occurs in shorter cycles. Also, half s bird's brain remains awake during sleep and it can control how deeply the other half sleeps.

It's not called the urban jungle for nothing. A city can be teeming with animals, from birds to bats to butterflies, and people who live there may be unaware of most.

That's because many animals that do choose to live where there are great concentrations of people eventually learn ways to live their lives without attracting notice.

There are some animals, though, that have the personality – and the agility – to live among people but to stay out of their way. Gray squirrels and pigeons can seem to be acrobats of urban and suburban sidewalks as they avoid being trampled.

Still other animals thrive in populated areas because they are terrific survivors. Norway rats and German cockroaches, two species people especially dislike, have managed to survive despite the most intense efforts imaginable to eliminate them.

But even in urban areas, there can be rural landscapes in the form of city parks. They are often havens for animals. For birds especially, a park's greenery can be an oasis in the middle of a desert of concrete and steel. In fact, concentrations of some birds can be higher in a good-sized park than they are in the outlying rural areas.

That's especially true in spring and fall when birds migrate. They have to stop and rest periodically, and if they are flying over a densely populated area with lots of buildings and little greenery, a park will stand out for them like the bull's-eye of a target. Branch Brook Park in Newark and Hudson County Park in Bayonne can be birdwatchers' paradises during the migration seasons.

Suburban towns can also harbor vast populations of wild animals. Some

House sparrow nest

Peregrine falcon at an urban nest

animals, such as deer, skunks, raccoons and opossums, are attracted by the easily obtained food provided by bird feeders, vegetable gardens, compost piles and trash cans.

Black bears have become an increasing problem in New Jersey, where they have been reported in every county at one time or another. When the bruins emerge from dormancy and food is still scarce, they may invade cities and suburbs farther east in search of bird feeders in particular.

For some animals, the feeding opportunities in cities can be greater than in the deep forest. Peregrine falcons were originally a mountain species that vanished from the state due to use of the pesticide DDT, which was eventually banned. They would build their nests on cliff ledges and use that vantage point to spot prey, usually other birds, which they would attack in flight. Falcons have since returned, but now they prefer the man-made cliffs of cities, including those provided by buildings and bridges as their base for nesting.

With hunting banned in residential areas and their natural predators all but gone, wild turkeys, coyotes, deer and other animals have flourished in some suburban areas. Deer forage in gardens, raccoons rifle garbage cans and coyotes may prey on pets.

In Hillsdale in early 2016, a letter carrier became trapped in his truck by a roaming band of turkeys. In Hainesport Township in 2012, turkeys in a flock became so bold that they would attack cars on the street and residents on the sidewalk until feeding the wild birds had to be banned, a measure many communities with a turkey problem are adopting.

Gray squirrels have adapted to life in cities. In rural forests, they each claim territories of perhaps an acre or two and feed mainly on acorns and other nuts. In a city park, where food can be more plentiful, as many as 10 might live in a single acre. The urban squirrel's diet may include acorns, popcorn, peanuts and any other foods humans offer or leave behind.

Wild turkeys in a back yard

A red fox in the neighborhood

Impressionist painters would not have gotten far without wildflowers.

Wildflowers were art before there was art – dashes of color on canvases of windblown meadows, craggy mountainsides and darkened forest floors.

Many seem to have been named by poets – Jack-in-the-pulpit, Queen Anne's lace, butter and eggs, yellow lady's slipper.

But as unplanned as a scattering of wildflowers may seem, where and when they bloom and the colors and shapes they take follow a general logic. Much of that logic has to do with helping each species of wildflower find its own place in the world.

If all wildflowers bloomed at the same time, grew in the same soil and sunlight conditions and attracted the same pollinators, the fierce competition would mean that only a few species would survive. So wildflowers evolved to be specialists. Some grow only in wet areas, some grow only in dry areas. Some thrive in valleys and others on mountainsides. Some can grow where there is a lot of sunlight, as in a meadow, while others can grow where there is little of it, as on a forest floor.

To further reduce competition, wildflowers also evolved to bloom at different times of year. Common violets bloom from April to June, but most alters don't bloom until September or October.

The beauty of wildflowers is not something created to please the human eye. It actually evolved to appeal to pollinators – butterflies,

Blue flag iris

Wild lupine

bees, ants, moths and even small birds, such as hummingbirds. The splashy and bold colors of some wildflowers are like neon signs outside a row of stores that aim to catch the eyes of passing customers. The fragrances the flowers give off and the sweet nectar produced inside the flowers are also intended as attractions to pollinators.

A wildflower must get the pollen that the male part of the flower creates to the female part of another wildflower of the same species so that seeds can be created. Pollinators are the pollen carriers.

If a butterfly visits a flower to feed on the nectar deep inside the flower, tiny grains of pollen may stick to it and be carried to the next flower it visits.

The varied shapes and colors of wildflowers also evolved to let a pollinator know exactly what kind of flower it is visiting. Most pollinators can recognize certain shapes and patterns of color, so if they like the nectar they find at a flower, they will know to visit that same type of flower again. In this way, pollen from a buttercup has a way of getting to another buttercup, rather than ending up on a wild geranium.

The bull's-eye shape of many flowers evolved to guide the pollinator to the nectar. "Here it is – right at the center," this shape seems to say. Other wildflowers have a shape like the end of a trumpet for the same reason. "The nectar is right inside here – you can't miss it," this shape seems to say.

In New Jersey, there may be more than 1,500 species of wildflowers that can be found through the seasons.

•
Wildflower or weed?

There is no official definition for which is which. When people do not like a wildflower for some reason, they may think of it as a weed. Some people think dandelions are weeds because they can take over a lawn. But others like their colorful flowers and think of them as wildflowers. Oxeye daisies are a favorite wildflower of many, but they are thought of as unwanted weeds by dairy farmers because cows may refuse to graze on them.

Turk's-cap lily

Red clover

Fragrant water lily

Beautiful wildflowers

"Gather ye rosebuds while ye may," the poet urged.

A century ago, it was advice taken much too literally, as picking wildflowers was such a common and overindulged practice that it's a wonder some species survived at all.

Whether it was citizens gathering bouquets for household display or botanists and hobbyists picking for their personal collections, some of the rarest and most beautiful wildflowers in the state – such as orchids, like showy lady's slipper – were disappearing.

Today, awareness of endangered species laws and of conservation issues generally keeps indiscriminate picking

Pink lady's slipper

of wildflowers to a minimum. Few would say anything about someone plucking daisies or black-eyed Susans from a field, but collecting of any flower that appears the least bit uncommon would probably draw a disapproving gaze and possibly more.

Nevertheless, in New Jersey, nearly 17 percent of the native plants are endangered, and almost 39 percent are imperiled in some way, many because of loss of favored habitat. While killing an endangered animal, such as an eagle, might bring a stiff fine or even jail time, at present there is no actual legal protection of these endangered plants in New Jersey.

Beach roses (rosa rugosa) growing wild in beach dunes

Butter
and
eggs

Wild
columbine

Violets

Milkweed
buds

Spotted touch-me-not

CHECKLIST
Common wildflowers

Oxeye daisy
June – Aug.
1 – 3 in. wide
☐

Daisy fleabane
May – July
1 in. wide
☐

Queen Anne's lace
June – Oct.
2 – 6 in. wide
(cluster width)
☐

Fragrant water lily
June – Sept.
3 – 6 in. wide
☐

Tall goldenrod
Aug. – Oct.
.2 in. long
☐

Common dandelion
April – Oct.
1.5 in. wide
☐

Black-eyed Susan
June – Oct.
2 – 3 in. wide
☐

Common buttercup
May – June
1 in. wide
☐

Marsh marigold
April – May
1 – 1.5 in. wide
☐

Butter and eggs
July – Oct.
1 – 2 in. long
☐

Day lily
June – Aug.
3 – 4 in. wide
☐

Jewelweed
July – Oct.
1 in. long
☐

Wild columbine
April – June
2 in. long
☐

Red clover
May – Oct.
1 in. wide
☐

Bull thistle
July – Sept.
1 – 2 in. wide
☐

Purple loosestrife
June – Sept.
6 – 12 in. long
☐

Common milkweed
June – Aug.
.5 in. wide
☐

Common blue violet
April – June
.5 – 1 in. wide
☐

Pickerelweed
July – Oct.
4 – 6 in.
☐

Spotted Joe-pye weed
Aug. – Sept.
4 – 5 in. wide
☐

Wild lupine
May – July
.7 in. long
☐

Wild geranium
May – June
1 – 2 in. wide
☐

Smooth aster
Sept. – Oct.
1 in. wide
☐

Skunk cabbage
March – May
3 – 6 in. long
☐

Cattail
June – Sept.
6 in. long
☐

Jack-in-the-pulpit
May – June
3 – 4 in. long
☐

A great spangled fritillary drinking in nectar at a flower

Flower power

The nectar of the gods. For hummingbirds, butterflies, bees and a range of other pollinating wildlife, the sweet liquid contained inside many flowers is truly that. Indeed, for many of them, flower nectar provides most of their fuel for energy.

Made up of a combination of water and different kinds of sugar, nectar is produced in parts of the flower called nectaries.

Plants need to spread their seeds to spread their species, so pollen from the male part – the stamen – of one plant must reach the female part – the pistil – of another to create a seed. Flowers produce nectar as a way to lure pollinating wildlife, such as butterflies and hummingbirds. Bits of pollen will stick to them while they are drinking, then they may visit another plant of the same kind for nectar and transfer the pollen to that plant's pistil as they linger to feed.

Butterflies drink nectar by sucking it in through a long narrow tube called a proboscis – like a drinking straw – that stays curled up at their mouth when they are not feeding.

A bumblebee

Hummingbirds and bees use their tongues to lap up the sweet liquid. A hummingbird's tongue may be nearly the length of its head when extended, and it may shoot out 13 times a second while drinking. Honey bees take nectar back to the hive where it is converted to honey.

Most adult butterflies die before winter, but a few, including the monarch, migrate. Monarchs depend on the sugars in nectar to make what can be an 1,800 mile flight to their wintering grounds in Mexico. The monarchs born in late summer, in the last generation of the season, have a small area of fatty tissue by their abdomen in which they store fat that has been converted from the sugar of nectar. It is that fat that helps sustain them on their migration and through the winter.

Hummingbirds, which might beat their wings 50 times a second while hovering at a flower, have the highest heart rate of any animal, sometimes 1,200 beats per minute while feeding (compared to perhaps 180 for a human who is exercising.) To power that extreme metabolism, hummingbirds have to drink a lot of energy-rich nectar, sometimes taking in their body weight in the liquid each day.

A monarch butterfly feeding

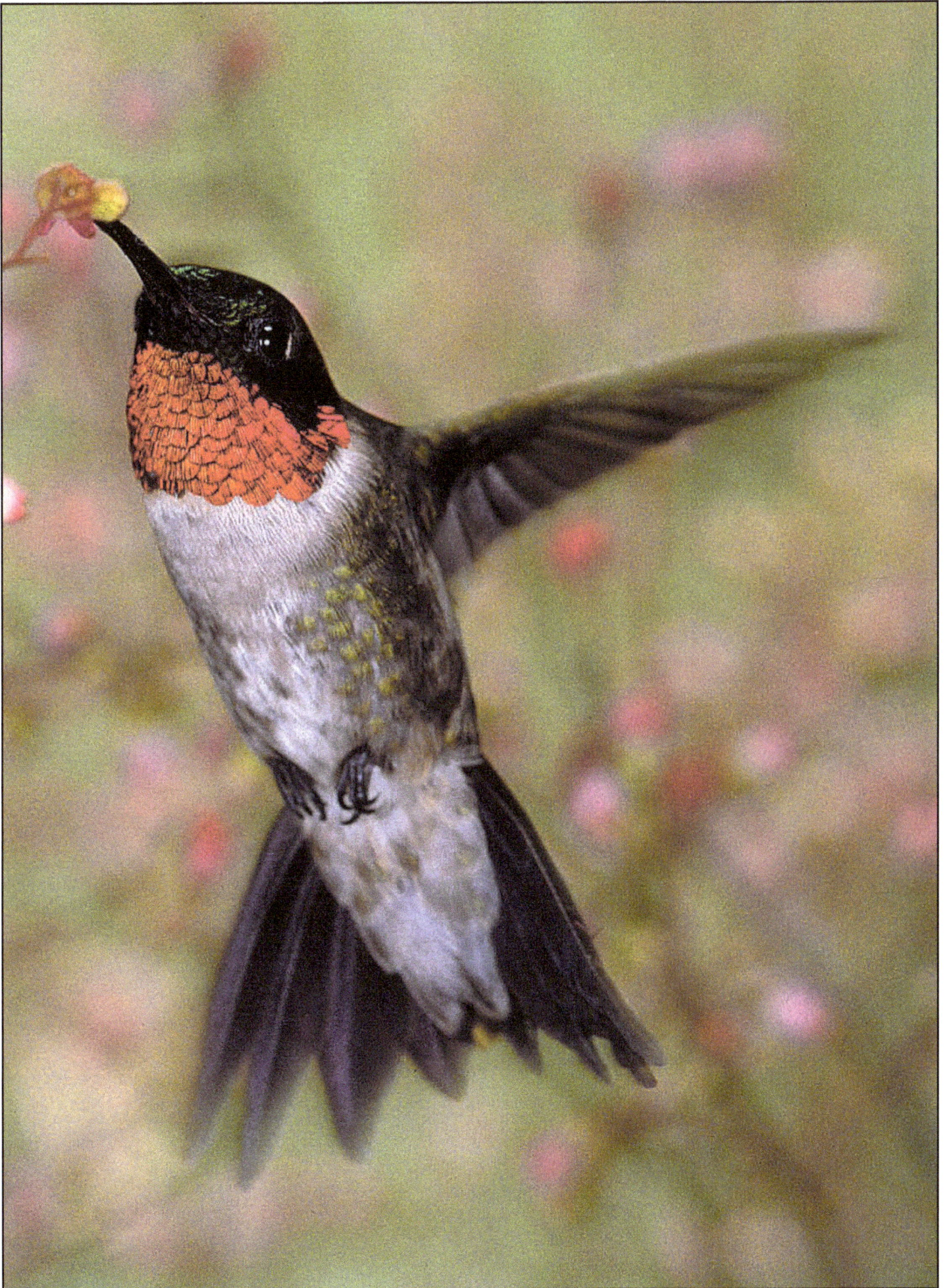

Ruby-throated hummingbird, male

Mushrooms – A fungus among us

There is a saying: "There are old mushroom hunters and bold mushroom hunters, but there are no old, bold mushroom hunters."

After a warm rain, lawns can turn into bountiful mushroom factories, as puffballs, shaggy manes and boletes sprout seemingly overnight. One may be tempted to look on these fungal colonies (a mushroom is indeed only an elaborate fungus) as a free source of something you would have to otherwise pay for in a supermarket. But experts warn against it, given that so many are poisonous.

There may be several thousand species of mushrooms to be found in New Jersey, including some that are deadly. There may be 10,000 species of mushrooms growing throughout North America, of which about 250 are considered edible, and about the same number are known to be poisonous, sickening or even capable of killing those who eat them. The rest are, to varying degrees, still mysteries.

Among the poisonous mushrooms, there are about 10 North American varieties that are considered deadly. And among those, the most feared is Amanita phalloides, the "death cap," which, although rare, has been found growing in suburban yards in the Northeast and elsewhere.

Its name is not hype. Eating just an ounce can be fatal.

Compounding the problem is that there are some poisonous mushrooms that can look very much like edible varieties. For instance, the destroying angel, which is deadly poisonous, can look almost identical to a type of common meadow mushroom.

The rule of thumb is that unless you know it, don't eat it.

Death cap mushroom, 3 in. tall

Orange oak bolete

Reg-veil amanita

Fly agaric

Ling chih

Russula Emetica

Even living within the heart of a city, you don't have to travel far in New Jersey to find a rural landscape in the form of a state park.

The state oversees some 441,000 acres of forests, beaches, bike trails, lakes, ponds, picnic areas, ski trails, streams, camping areas, old-growth trees, waterfalls, lodges, cabins, fishing spots, hiking trails and rivers – nearly 8 percent of the state's total land area.

There are 39 parks, 11 forests, three recreational areas and 43 natural areas in the state system, ranking New Jersey eighth in the nation and second in the Northeast in the acreage of its state park system.

Statue of Liberty, visible from Liberty State Park

Some notable state forests and parks in New Jersey

Liberty State Park in Jersey City, at 1,212 acres, sits across Upper New York Bay from Ellis Island, Liberty Island and the Statue of Liberty, connecting to them by ferry service. The park has miles of paved walks with dramatic views of the Manhattan skyline. The park is also home to the "Empty Sky" 9/11 Memorial honoring those who died in the 2001 attack on the World Trade Center.

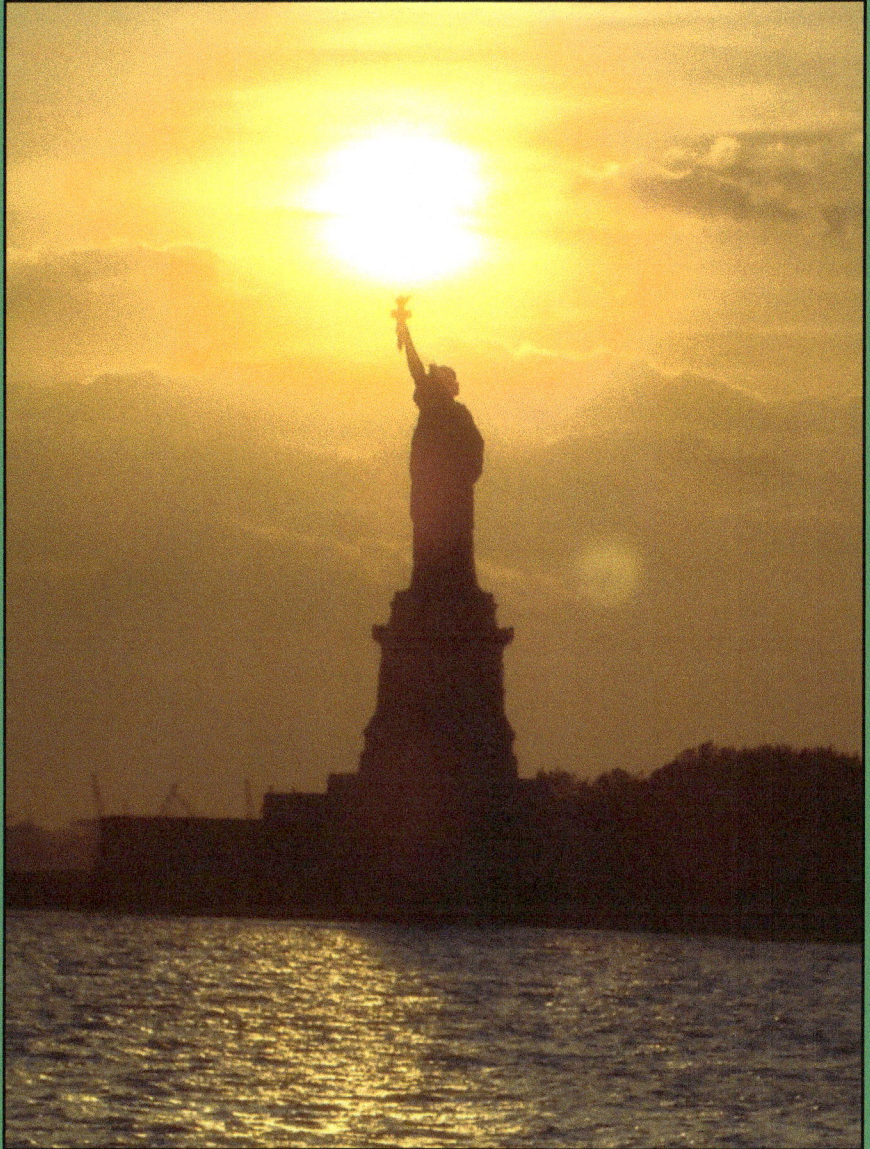

High Point State Park in Sussex is nearly 16,091 acres. The park is home to High Point, the 1,803-foot peak that is, appropriately, the highest point in New Jersey and on the long ridge of Kittatinny Mountain. With nearly 50 miles of hiking trails (including a portion of the Appalachian Trail), the park is a favorite of hikers.

Wharton State Forest is 122,880 acres spread over Atlantic, Burlington and Camden counties. The largest state forest in New Jersey, it is also home to Batsto Village, a historic iron and glass manufacturing site that dates to the 1760s. The entire forest is located within the pine barrens, a distinctive area marked by poor soils and stunted trees, mostly pines.

Cape May Point State Park in Cape May Point, at 244 acres, is considered one of the best spots in North America to view the fall migration of birds, from gulls and goldfinches to sparrows and sapsuckers. There are nature trails as well as an elevated platform and boardwalks to aid in wildlife viewing. And the 157-foot Cape May lighthouse is a landmark.

Island Beach State Park in Berkeley township is 3,003 acres. The 10-mile-long undeveloped barrier beach is one of the last of its kind on the north Atlantic coast. With its sandy beaches, the park is popular for swimming, and with its maritime forests, sand dunes, marshes and tidal pools, the park is a favorite for wildlife watchers. Fishing from the beaches is also popular.

In the early 1800s New Jersey may have looked much like a farm state in the Midwest. Farm fields, barren of trees, stretched from horizon to horizon in many places.

Native Americans who lived in New Jersey found they could more easily hunt animals in open areas than in thick forests, so they burned away many of the trees and shrubs. And when Europeans settled in the state, they cleared more of the trees to create farm fields.

After the Civil War, though, many farmers in New Jersey and the Northeast decided to leave their farms because they found they could not make a profit due to competition from farmers in the Midwest. Some moved west, seeking better land. Others moved to cities, seeking other kinds of jobs. Gradually, open land in the state began to grow back into forests.

Today, even though New Jersey is the most densely populated state in the nation, about 2 millions acres, 42 percent of all the state's land, is forested.

Surely, there are million upon millions of trees in the state – too many trees to possibly count. Not true. Just as it takes a census of people periodically, the federal government also takes an inventory of trees. In 2014, it was estimated there were 894 million trees in the state that are at least one inch in diameter at breast height.

New Jersey, with its diverse geology and land features, from coasal beaches to the vast pine barrens to the northwest highlands, has a tremendous variety of tree species in its forests, but where different trees grow depends largely on the soil. Trees need soil to anchor their roots and provide nutrients to help them grow. As the type and depth of soil changes from region to region, so will the trees you see.

In the mountainous region of the Northwest, where the soils are rich, you will find many tall oaks and hickories. In the pine barrens in central New Jersey, where the soils are sandy and poor in nutrients, you will see mainly pitch pines, which tend to grow lower to the ground.

Over the years, though, forest fires, tree diseases and insects have dramatically altered the state's forestland. Because the pine barrens were largely uninhabited, forest fires would often burn out of control, raging over thousands of acres at a time and limiting the age and size of the trees that would grow there.

In Colonial times, the American Chestnut, which produced tasty nuts as well as wood that was especially good for building, was essential to the economy of the Northeast. Perhaps four billion chestnuts grew from Maine to Mississippi. However, a blight caused by a fungus virtually wiped the chestnuts out starting in the early 1900s.

Similarly, the stately American elm, which lined the streets of many American communities, was nearly wiped out by fungus in the mid-1900s. One of the only stands of elms that was resistant to the disease was found lining the entrance road of Princeton University, and many efforts to restore the elms nationally depend on cuttings taken from those trees.

Gypsy moths, insects that eat tree leaves, particularly those of oaks, have also done considerable damage in the state. In 1981, nearly 800,000 acres of forestland were stripped of leaves by the moths.

Dominant forest types of New Jersey

- Oak and hickory
- Maple, beech and birch
- Elm, ash and cottonwood
- Oak, blackgum and cypress
- Oak and pine
- Pitch and shortleaf pine

Forest makeup of New Jersey

Number of trees above 4.9 in. in diameter at breast height, 2014 estimate

Pitch pine (20.1%); Red maple (16.2%); Atlantic white cedar (7%); Black gum (6.5%); White oak (5.7%); All other species (44.5%)

CHECKLIST
Common trees

Sugar maple
typical height
60 – 80 ft.
☐

Red maple
50 – 80 ft.
☐

Northern
red oak
60 – 80 ft.
☐

Chestnut oak
60 – 80 ft.
☐

Sweet birch
60 – 80 ft.
☐

Paper birch
50 – 70 ft.
☐

Black cherry
50 – 70 ft.
☐

American
beech
60 – 80 ft.
☐

Black gum
60-80 ft.
☐

Green ash
40 – 60 ft.
☐

Weeping
willow
30 – 50 ft.
☐

White oak
80-100 ft.
☐

Atlantic white
cedar
40-60 ft.
☐

Pitch pine
50 – 70 ft.
☐

Street trees

Honeylocust
50 – 80 ft.
☐

Norway
maple
40 – 60 ft.
☐

London
planetree
70 – 90 ft.
☐

Red maple

Apple

Sugar maple

Eastern white pine

Norway Spruce

Seed science

The apple doesn't fall far from the tree, the saying goes. However, for a species of tree to survive and spread, there has to be a way for the seeds to travel some distance to new locations.

The seeds of an apple tree are contained in the apple and when animals eat the lucious fruits, they inadvertently provide a way for the seeds to travel to a new place – usually in their digestive tract. When the animal finally passes solid wastes, the seeds encased in a hard shell end up on the ground, ready to take root, amid ready-made fertilizer.

Some trees, like red and sugar maples, produce winged seeds that travel on the wind to distant places like miniature helicopters. Other trees, like American beeches, produce tasty nuts (tasty to humans also) that are seeds as well. The acorns of oak trees are also seeds.

Coniferous trees, like pines, hemlocks and spruces, produce edible cones with the seeds inside. When a squirrel or other cone-eating animal carries the cone a distance to eat it, the seeds have a chance to travel too.

Pitch pine

Eastern hemlock

Northern red oak

American beech

Yellow birch

An acorn from a northern red oak pushes out a taproot

An acorn that drops to the ground in autumn will grow a main root, called a taproot, that pushes down into the soil once temperatures warm in the spring. Within a week the root may be several inches long. Within another week, a stem may begin to grow upward and leaves will soon appear on the stem.

Because so many acorns are eaten or do not fall in a place where they can germinate, it may take 500 acorns to produce one oak seedling that reaches a year old.

Acorn Ecology

The tiny acorns that litter the ground on hiking trails in the fall can be the key to survival for many forms of wildlife in a forest ecosystem. After all, mighty oaks from little acorns grow. And on little acorns a range of animals feed, including black bears, deer, turkeys, squirrels, chipmunks, mice, blue jays and vaious insects. And many of the animals that don't feed on acorns feed on animals that do. The nut-eating animals are often prey for larger animals, such as foxes, coyotes, bobcats, hawks and owls.

However, if all the acorns that fell in autumn got eaten, there would be no mighty oaks, and if there were no mighty oaks, the populations of all those animals that depend on acorns, either directly or indirectly, would be in trouble. So oaks have evolved to have a fascinating strategy that ensures that both oaks and animals survive.

An acorn still on the branch

Oaks have years when they produce a huge crop of acorns, called mast years. For oaks, mast years occur every three to five years on average. But in the years between mast years, oaks may produce few if any acorns. That way, the populations of the acorn-eating animals have less food in the in-between years and can never grow so large that all the acorns get eaten in the mast years. That guarantees new oaks will be able to take root while allowing the animals that depend on acorns to survive.

But here is the fascinating part. If one oak had a mast year and the oak beside it did not, this process would not work. Acorn eaters would still have enough food that their populations would grow without limit, and in mast years, all the acorns might get eaten. But that doesn't happen.

In one of the great mysteries of nature, oaks, and other nut-bearing trees, have evolved so that somehow mast years occur at the same time for trees of that species over a vast area, sometimes thousands of square miles. That means the population of the oaks and the animals that eat acorns and other nuts remain in balance, and all have a chance to survive.

Oaks can't communicate with each other, as far as anyone knows. So how do they all agree to grow so many acorns at the same time? One leading theory is that variations in seasonal temperature, especially in the spring, trigger trees over a large area to produce large or small crops of nuts. One study of oaks in California found that in warm, dry Aprils, acorn production tended to be high in the fall.

They are the silent observers of history. The oldest living trees in New Jersey were alive when Native Americans dominated the region, when the Revolutionary War was fought and when electric lights first appeared.

Some of the state's ancient trees may be 500 and possibly 600 years old. However, very little virgin forest still exists in New Jersey. Natural and manmade fires in the extensive pine barrens region destroyed pines, oaks and other trees there that might have qualified as old-growth. And clearing for homes and businesses as well as the cutting of trees for fuel and industry has eliminated other older trees throughout the state. So only about 400 to 500 acres of true old-growth forest are known to exist in New Jersey.

The largest stand of old-growth trees in the state is in Bear Swamp, state-owned lands in Cumberland County in southwestern New Jersey. It's estimated there are about 215 acres of black gums, red maples, American beeches, tulip trees and white oaks.

However, if you think that the oldest trees in a forest are always the largest trees, you'd be wrong. Perhaps the oldest trees in New Jersey are some of the most inconspicuous, usually growing to a height of less than 80 feet. They are black gum trees, also called black tupelo or pepperidge trees.

In Colonial times, as so much forestland was being cleared for farming, many black gums were spared cutting as they often grew in swampy places, such as Bear Swamp, and were not considered of any value.

Only in recent years have people who study old-growth trees recognized just how long this wetland species can survive. For many years it was thought that the oldest trees in the Northeast were no more than 550 years old. However, in 1996 in New Hampshire, a black gum was found that is now estimated to be nearly 680 years old.

Also growing to an impressive age are white oaks. One in Salem and another in Basking Ridge may be 500 to 600 years old.

How do scientists determine the age of a tree? By counting its rings. A tree grows new wood around the outside of its trunk each year. In the late spring and early summer, when there is usually more moisture in the ground, the wood is light in appearance. In late summer and early fall, when conditions are usually drier, the wood being added tends to be darker. This alternating light and dark wood creates rings that can be seen when the tree falls in a storm or is cut.

To count the rings of a living tree, a scientist drills out a pencil-thin "core," a rod of wood extracted from the trunk on which the rings can be seen.

There is no firm definition for an old-growth tree, but for many species, living 150 to 200 years can put them in that category. Most old-growth trees in the Northeast are found in the higher elevations of mountains or in places that people can't easily reach, such as on steep slopes.

While 600 years is an impressive life span for a tree in New Jersey, it wouldn't raise an eyebrow in some other regions. There is a bald cypress in North Carolina that is estimated to be 1,650 years old, the champion for old growth in the East.

The champions for the nation, and perhaps the world, are bristlecone pines that grow on the barren, windy slopes of the southwestern United States. Some of those may be nearly 5,000 years old.

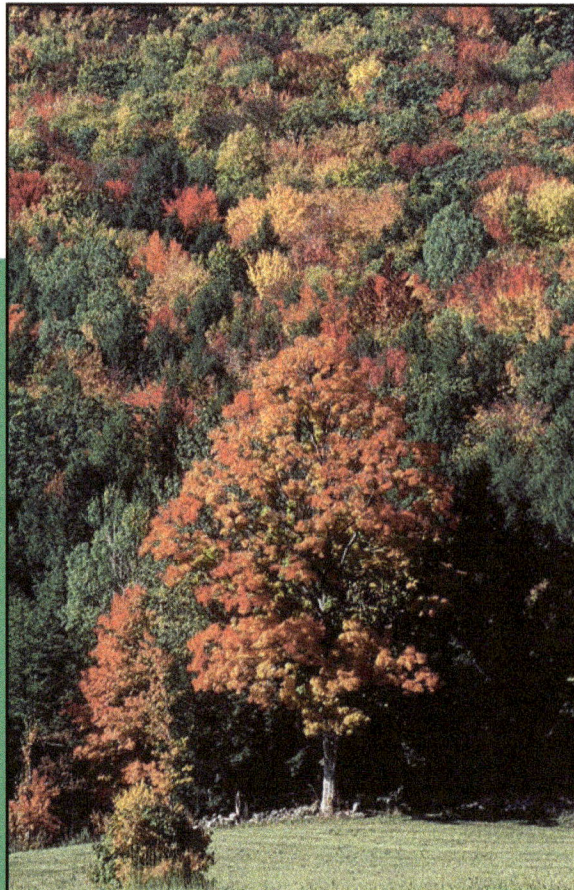

Is fall foliage just an accident?

Perhaps nature's most brilliant artistic touch, the scarlets and golds of autumn leaves may also be one of nature's most beautiful accidents.

The startling colors of fall are certainly admired by human beings. But the colors seem to defy one of nature's primary laws, since they are of no use to the trees themselves.

Most plants and animals have the features they have because those features help them survive in the world. But what use is a colorful leaf to a tree in autumn since the leaf is just about to die and fall to the ground?

Some scientists believe that autumn colors may have begun as an accident, the unexpected result of the chemical changes a tree goes through as it prepares to lose its leaves each fall.

But even if it was an accident, since this coloring causes no harm to the trees, there is no reason for trees to lose this process. If the coloring did cause harm, those species of trees whose leaves changed color might have become extinct by now, and only the trees whose leaves didn't change color might be alive today.

Snowy egrets in their nest

Imagine mountains as high as Mount Everest. Imagine erupting volcanoes. Imagine mile-high glaciers or frozen snowswept plains.

You are imagining landscapes that could have been seen in the Northeast at different times in its history.

Hard to believe? Not for geologists. They know that the appearance of every region on Earth has changed over time. They also know that now is a quiet time in the geologic cycle of New Jersey and the Northeast, a momentary calm amid the violent upheavals that have marked the history of the region's landscape.

The Earth's crust, or surface layer, is made up of vast rock plates that form the continents and the ocean floor. There are about a dozen large plates and many smaller ones covering the Earth's surface, arranged like pieces in a jigsaw puzzle.

The crust under the oceans may have an average thickness of just four or five miles. The crust of the continental plates is about 25 miles thick on average.

Essentially, the plates "float" on a layer of denser rock, called the mantle, deeper within the Earth. The Earth's core has a temperature of perhaps 10,800 degrees Fahrenheit, and this great heat creates circulating currents of molten rock within the mantle, which slowly push the crustal plates along.

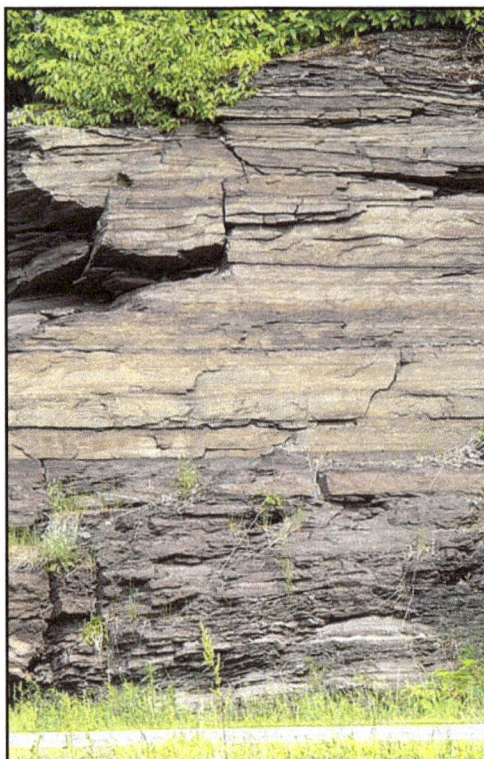

Layers of sedimentary rock in exposed bedrock by a highway

The plates typically move a few inches a year, sometimes coming together and sometimes moving apart. This is called continental drift.

Even at such a slow speed, though, when these massive plates push against each other, geologic fireworks happen. Mountains gradually rise into the air, volcanoes may erupt and earthquakes might rumble.

That's what's happening currently in the western United States. The Pacific and North American plates are slowly sliding by each other, grinding together along their edges. About 65 million years ago, when the plates were pushing right into each other, this process created the Rocky Mountains, which are considered "young" mountains. (Scientists believe the Earth is about 4.6 billion years old.)

New Jersey is also part of the North American plate, but for nearly 200 million years this plate has been separating from the plate that is next to it on the east, the one on which Africa is located. So there are no strong geologic pressures on New Jersey's part of the plate to create or enlarge mountains, or to produce volcanoes or sizable earthquakes, in the Northeast.

Boundaries of major plates of the Earth's crust

North American plate

Pacific plate

Cocos plate

Caribbean plate

Nazca plate

South American plate

Arabian plate

Eurasian plate

Pacific plate

African plate

Philippine plate

Indian-Australian plate

Antarctic plate   Scotia plate   Antarctic plate

Drifting continents

At least three times in the last 500 million years, the East Coast of North America collided with other continental plates. These collisions did much to shape the landscape of New Jersey.

Although continental plates may move only inches a year, their masses are so great and the forces pushing them along are so powerful that the process has long-lasting momentum.

Once the plates come together they may continue to push against each other for millions of years. This can create huge mountains in the region of the collision or, if the reaction of the land is violent, earthquakes or volcanoes.

500 million years ago

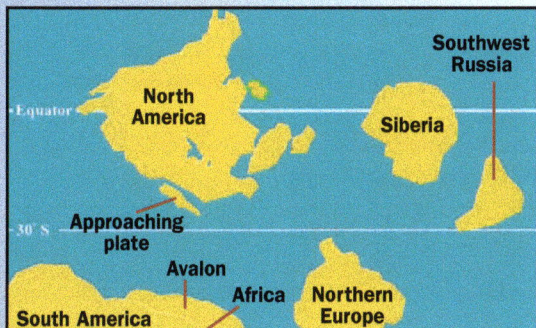

The land that will one day be New Jersey is lying on a continent at the equator, but it is underwater, covered by a shallow sea. Trees, plants and animals have not yet appeared on land. Primitive life is still developing in the oceans. The first fishlike creatures appear in water. Less than a foot in length, they lack jaws but they do have backbones, perhaps the first animals that are vertebrates.

The oxygen content of the Earth's atmosphere is rising sharply, but it will be another 100 million years before air-breathing land animals evolve.

Drifting north toward early North America is a plate, covered with volcanoes, that is about to collide with what will become the East Coast.

460 million years ago

The volcanic plate collides with the North American coast, pushing up layers of rock that form the original Appalachian Mountains and the New Jersey highlands in the northwest part of the state. Originally, these mountains were steeper than the Rocky Mountains today. However, rain falling on their slopes steadily erodes them and by 420 million years ago, New Jersey is again under a shallow inland sea.

Meanwhile, Avalon, another plate, has broken free of the united African-South American continent and is drifting north.

380 million years ago

Avalon collides with North America, creating massive mountains in eastern U.S. and Canada. When these peaks erode, rivers carrying debris deposit mud and sediment over surrounding lands. New Jersey is again covered by a shallow sea. Primitive fish now fill the seas, and plants are starting to flourish on land.

300 million years ago

200 million years ago

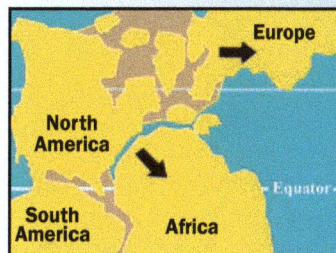

Africa collides with North America about 300 million years ago. All seven continents become joined in a single vast continent, called Pangaea by geologists. Layers of land in New Jersey are compressed and folded like an accordion. Those features can be seen today in the New Jersey highlands.

About 200 million years ago, Africa pulls away from North America.

The first dinosaurs appear about 230 million years ago, but they are relatively small, just a few feet in height. The first mammals, not much larger than mice, appear about the same time.

Ridge and Valley Province

African plate collides

New Jersey west to east

The rock cycle

Rocks have their own life cycle. It begins on the surface of the Earth when wind, rain and other natural forces break down existing rocks and other materials. The resulting particles become compressed and cemented together over the course of time to form new rocks.

When sand particles are turned to rock in this way, sandstone is the result. When clay, such as what is deposited on the bottom of a lake, is turned to rock, shale is the result. These two rocks are called sedimentary rocks, one of three categories of rocks along with metamorphic and igneous.

Eventually, sedimentary rocks, such as sandstone and shale, are buried by layers of other sedimentary rocks. With the heat and pressure deeper inside the Earth, they can become compressed further, making them harder still. That can turn them into metamorphic rocks, such as quartzite and slate.

Metamorphic rocks may eventually move to the surface due to earthquakes or the erosion of the land above them. But if metamorphic rocks move deeper into the Earth, the higher temperatures there can turn them to molten rock.

If this molten material hardens underground, it can become igneous rock, such as granite. If it surges up to the Earth's surface through a volcano as lava and hardens, it will become another form of igneous rock, such as basalt.

Harsh weather and the freezing and thawing through the seasons eventually disintegrate surface rocks. These rock particles may then become part of new sedimentary rocks, starting the cycle once again.

The rock collection

Sandstone
Sedimentary; formed from sand

Quartzite
Metamorphic; formed from sandstone

Shale
Sedimentary; formed from mud and clay

Limestone
Sedimentary; formed from minerals such as calcite

Siltstone
Sedimentary; formed from particles of silt, clay and sand

Slate
Metamorphic; formed from shale at low temperatures

Conglomerate
Sedimentary; formed from a mix of sand and pebbles

Marble
Metamorphic; formed from limestone

Schist
Metamorphic; often formed from shale at medium temperatures

Mineral or rock?

Minerals have crystalline structures, and they are usually made up of only a few chemical elements. For instance, diamond is made of carbon, and quartz is made of silicon and oxygen. Rocks, such as schist or granite, may be made up of combinations of minerals and bits of other rocks. While the minerals in it may have crystalline structures, the overall rock usually does not.

Gneiss
Metamorphic; formed from igneous and sedimentary rocks

Granite
Igneous; formed when molten rock cools underground

Quartz, a mineral

The bedrock of New Jersey

If you dig down through the loose dirt and rocks on the Earth's surface, you will eventually strike solid rock, called bedrock, that is often the same type of rock for miles around.

In coastal areas or on steep mountain slopes, you may not have to dig deeply at all to find bedrock. In river valleys, where flooding has deposited layer upon layer of silt and clay over the centuries, you may have to dig down a hundred feet or more.

The land masses that came together to form New Jersey over millions of years carried different kinds and ages of bedrock with them. Like different colors of modeling clay pushed together, the bedrock beneath the region is divided into zones of those different types of rock.

There were times in New Jersey's history when huge mountains rose up in eastern North America as the result of continental collisions. When those mountains eroded, vast amounts of sediment were washed into areas of present day New Jersey, forming certain kinds of bedrock. There were other times when much of the state was covered by shallow seas and the sediments deposited at the bottom of these waters eventually formed other kinds of bedrock. All of this gives the state great variation in its underlying geology.

Map code
Type of bedrock and its general age in millions of years

Sedimentary – Conglomerate, sandstone, shale, limestone – 359 to 420

Sedimentary – Conglomerate, sandstone, shale, limestone – 420 to 444

Sedimentary – Shale, limestone – 444 to 485

Sedimentary – Limestone, sandstone – 485 to 541

Metamorphic – Marble – About 1,050

Metamorphic and igneous – Gneiss and granite – More than 1,000

Sedimentary – Siltstone, shale, sandstone, conglomerate – 145 to 201

Igneous – Basalt – 145 to 201

Sedimentary – Siltstone, shale, sandstone, conglomerate – 200 to 250

Igneous – Diabase – 145 to 201

Sedimentary – Sand, silt and clay – 65-145

Sedimentary – Sand, silt and clay – 2.6 to 65

Sedimentary – Beach and estuary deposits – 12,000 years ago to the present

Fearfully great lizards: translated from Greek, that's what "dinosauria" actually means. For nearly 165 million years, from about 230 million years ago to 65 million years ago, these legendary beasts roamed the Earth.

Wherever you walk in North America, the fierce Tyrannosaurus rex and the massive Triceratops once walked. But while scientists find the bones of these ancient creatures in other regions, they find few of them in New Jersey.

However, one of the most famous discoveries of dinosaur bones – and the discovery that is credited with starting American dinosaur paleontology – took place in Haddonfield in1838. A local farmer, John Hopkins, found ancient bones of what appeared to be a very large animal while digging fertilizer in a pit near a river. However, it was another two decades before a geologist, William Foulke, who lived nearby, heard about the bones and pushed to have the digging in the pit resumed.

Eventually, about half the skeleton (minus the skull) of a dinosaur called a Hadrosaurus, a plant eater about 20 to 25 feet long, was unearthed. It was the most complete dinosaur skeleton ever found until that time. Once the bones were assembled and the missing bones recreated, it became the first dinosaur skeleton ever mounted in order to show what the animal (minus its flesh) looked like when it was alive. It finally went on display in Philadelphia in1868.

Since then, most dinosaur bones have been found in other regions. Bones are preserved as fossils when they are buried by sand or mud, which then turn to sedimentary rock. However, conditions in New Jersey were not ideal for preserving the sedimentary bedrock bearing these fos-

A pair of Diplodocuses watch a Pterodactyl soar overhead, a scene that likely depicts a shoreline in what is now western North America in the late Jurassic Period

The Haddonfield Hadrosaurus

sils. For most of the last 200 million years ago, the surface rocks of the state have been worn down by rain and wind, a process called erosion. However, geologists do find fossilized footprints of dinosaurs in New Jersey.

A rock bearing the footprint of a dinosaur is like a photograph that is millions of years old. It's a snapshot in stone of events of perhaps one warm summer morning by the shores of an ancient river or lake. A dinosaur might have wandered down to the edge of the water to drink, pressing its feet into the soft mud created by a rainstorm the evening before. In the hot sun, the mud and prints dried and hardened and were buried by other layers of mud containing still more dinosaur prints.

Over the centuries, the buried layers and prints would turn to rock such as shale. Erosion and earthquakes even-

The age of dinosaurs

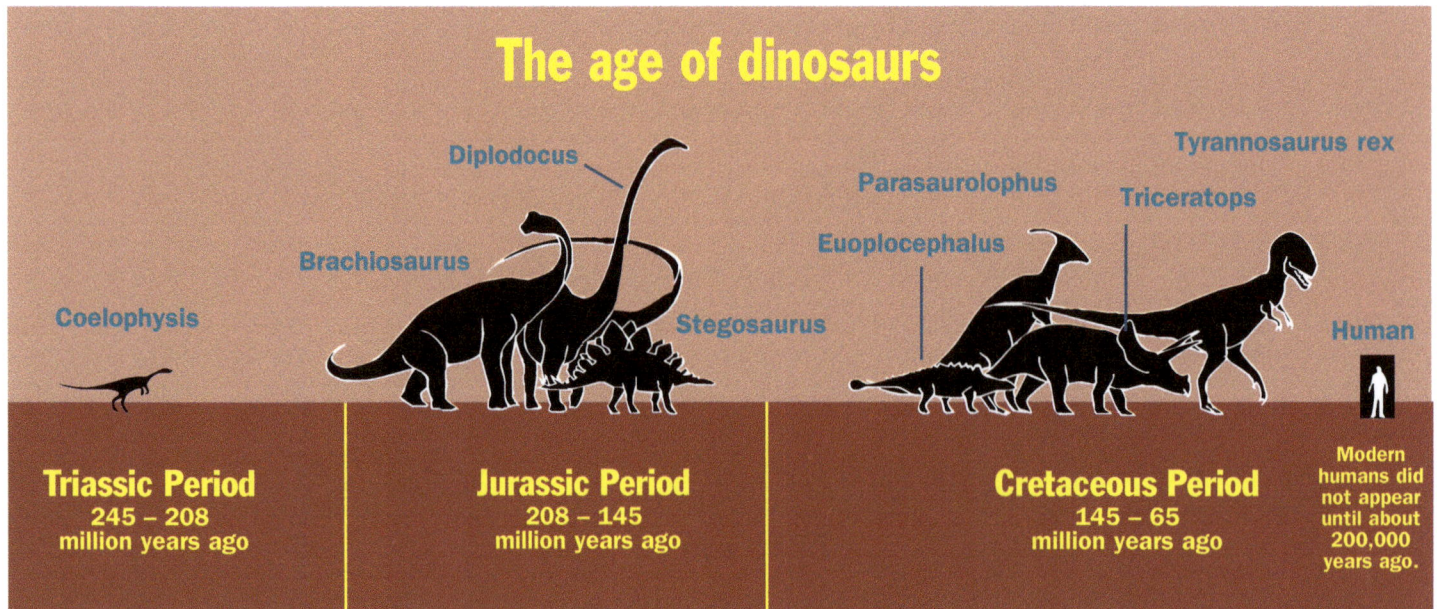

Coelophysis

Brachiosaurus

Diplodocus

Stegosaurus

Euoplocephalus

Parasaurolophus

Triceratops

Tyrannosaurus rex

Human

Triassic Period
245 – 208
million years ago

Jurassic Period
208 – 145
million years ago

Cretaceous Period
145 – 65
million years ago

Modern humans did not appear until about 200,000 years ago.

How dinosaur footprints were formed
The Newark Basin about 190 to 200 million years ago

Erosion created a constant flow of sediments off surrounding mountains

River

Newark Basin

Rift valleys

1. Tracks left by a dinosaur in soft mud after a rain storm might dry and harden in the hot sun over several days.

2. Another rain storm might wash a new layer of mud over the footprints, filling them in. Then this layer might fill with new footprints and harden in the sun.

3. Over time, layer would build upon layer, and the original tracks might be hundreds of feet underground, where they would turn to rock under the pressure.

tually brought some of the footprint-bearing rocks back to the surface, allowing a geologist to crack apart the layers to reveal the tracks, like someone turning the pages of a photo album.

From about 200 to 190 million years ago, conditions in what is today called the Newark Basin were just right for creating fossilized tracks.

As the African continent struggled to pull apart from North America, a series of valleys, called rift valleys, was formed in the United States from Massachusetts down

Dinosaur print

to North Carolina as the land was ripped apart, a false start for the eventual separation that would come farther to the east and create the Atlantic Ocean. One such valley going through what is today New Jersey filled with mud, and dinosaurs left their footprints before the mud hardened.

However, that era was in the early part of the age of dinosaurs, before the larger and better known of their breed, such as Tyrannosaurus rex, had developed. So the footprints that have been found in New Jersey are from relatively small Triassic Period dinosaurs, such as the Coelophysis, which was about the size of a large ostrich.

Earth's history

Earth forms and the outer crust solidifies about 4.6 billion years ago

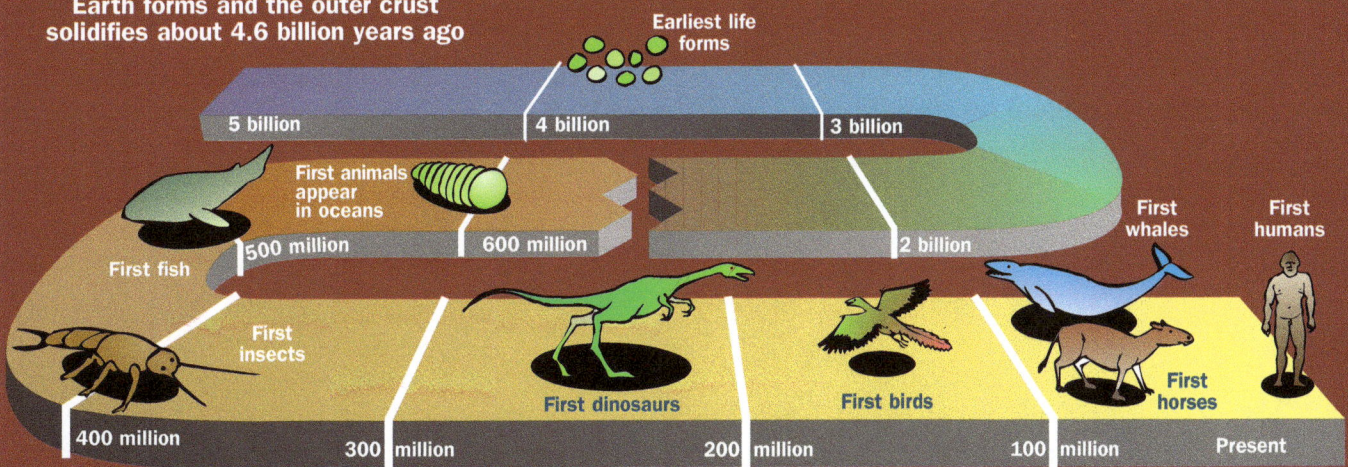

Earliest life forms

5 billion   4 billion   3 billion

First animals appear in oceans

500 million   600 million   2 billion

First fish

First whales

First humans

First insects

First dinosaurs   First birds   First horses

400 million   300 million   200 million   100 million   Present

It was the dead of winter even in the heart of summer. It was the ice age.

During the last two million years, there have been four major advances of continental glaciers into the northern United States from centers in Canada.

The most recent ice age began about 70,000 years ago when a glacier that had formed in eastern Canada slowly expanded, eventually covering most of the Northeast United States. In some places, the ice was more than a mile thick. The glacier, called by geologists the Laurentide ice sheet, also spread west, covering most of Canada and the northernmost United States from the Rocky Mountains eastward. It did not finally melt away from New Jersey until about 17,000 years ago.

Glaciers form when the climate of a region cools enough so that snow builds up in winter faster than it melts in summer. Just as a snowball turns to an ice ball if you squeeze it hard enough, snow, if it continues to pile up, can eventually become so compressed that much of it turns to ice, especially at the bottom of the pile.

The increase in snow and ice year after year can create a mound of ice so high that the weight of it causes the ice to begin to spread slowly outward at the bottom, like thick maple syrup flowing on a tabletop – except at a much slower pace. On average, a glacier may advance a few feet a day. But at times, it may barely move and at other times it may surge forward several hundred feet in a day.

Even at this relatively slow speed, though, a glacier can move a great distance over thousands of years, as it did during the last ice age.

Much of the landscape of northern New Jersey was shaped by the glaciers that reached down into the Northeast. The ice covered even High Point, reaching a height of perhaps 2,000 feet above the land.

A glacier can be like a vacuum cleaner, drawing up into the ice the rocks and boulders that it finds in its path or that it digs out of the bedrock as it advances. When at last the climate warms enough so that a glacier begins to melt back, all the debris trapped in the ice is dropped to the ground, and that is why the northern counties had so many loose rocks and boulders on the surface.

Sometimes a rock of one type is droped in an area of bedrock of another kind. These rocks are called erratics.

A family of woolly mammoths during the ice age.

Bear Rock and Tripod Rock on Pyramid Mountain in Morris County are erratics. Tripod Rock is particulary interesting since it is a large boulder perched on three smaller ones. For Native Americans and early European settlers in the region, its origin must have been quite a mystery.

As a glacier begins to melt, large chunks may break off. Because of the chunks' huge weight, they may depress the land on which they sit. Later, when the chunks melt, the meltwater may fill these depressions, creating lakes, which geologists call kettle lakes. Lake Grinnell in Sussex County and Franklin Lake in Passaic County are kettle lakes.

Once the ice was gone from New Jersey, the landscape did not immediately spring back to life. It was probably frozen, barren and blanketed with snow much of the year, a wasteland covered with glacial debris. Low tundra vegetation, similar to what you would see near the Arctic today, grew on it for centuries. However, many of the animals and plants that are native to the region today gradually began to spread their range from the south into this area. The animals included deer, skunks and black bears.

The first human beings arriving in the Northeast after the last ice age may have encountered very cold conditions indeed.

Stone walls, legacy of the ice age

It's an astonishing mystery if you don't know the explanation. Rock walls running through the middle of a highland forest. Who could have toiled to construct lines of carefully stacked rocks running from nowhere to nowhere? The answer is: the region's earliest European farmers.

Much of northern New Jersey was covered with a massive glacier 25,000 years ago. However, the glacier eventually melted away and humans moved in. When early European farmers went to clear their land to plant crops, they found that the soil was littered with rocks and boulders dropped by the glacier as it melted.

So in the highlands, the Kittatinny Valley and elsewhere, the stone walls were permanent fences around fields, but they were also trash piles for all the rocks and boulders the farmers found.

After the Civil War, many of those early farms were abandoned as agriculture moved west. The farm houses disappeared, the fields turned to forests, but the walls remain.

North America's last glacier
(about 20,000 years ago)

Cordilleran ice sheet

Laurentide ice sheet

THE FUTURE CANADA

Glacier

New Jersey

THE FUTURE UNITED STATES

Animals of the ice age

Giant cats with teeth like daggers. Shaggy-coated, long-tusked creatures that looked like elephants. Beavers larger than a man. Bison weighing a ton and a half. Musk oxen, ground sloths, wild pigs and caribou.

Some of the animals that roamed North America as the last ice age ended may have seemed to belong more to the age of dinosaurs. The much colder climate of the northern parts of the continent 20,000 years ago provided a home to a different group of animals than one sees today, creatures that were able to survive on a frozen landscape.

However, as the ice melted away and the climate warmed, many of the same animals found in the

Northeast today, including skunks, white-tailed deer, opossums, raccoons and black bears, moved into the region from warmer areas to the south.

It's believed the first humans arrived in North America between 13,000 and 14,000 years ago as the last ice age was ending. They may have hunted the largest of the ancient ice age animals to extinction in a matter of just 2,000 or 3,000 years, including the woolly mammoths and mastodons.

Saber-toothed cats are believed to have lived throughout North and South America. These huge predators, which also hunted mammoths and mastodons, probably went extinct soon after the ice age ended, when their primary prey disappeared.

Woolly mammoth
Height: 9 to 11 feet at the shoulder
Weight: 8,000 to 12,000 pounds

American mastodon
Height: 8 to 10 feet at the shoulder
Weight: 8,000 to 10,000 pounds

Saber-toothed cat
Length: 6 to 8 feet
Weight: 400 to 500 pounds

The first Americans may have been a small band of hunters traveling in search of caribou or woolly mammoths more than 13,000 years ago who had no idea of the history they were about to make.

During the last ice age, so much of the Earth's water was ice that the surface of the ocean may have been more than 300 feet lower than it is today. As a result, a temporary land bridge emerged connecting Asia to Alaska. Human beings had already spread through much of Europe, Africa and Asia, but North America may still have been uninhabited by people.

The earliest North Americans may have entered Alaska from 17,000 to 40,000 years ago, but found their way south blocked by massive glaciers. However, it's believed that about 14,000 to 16,000 years ago, the climate warmed enough that a passage opened in the ice sheets allowing them to travel south into what is today the American Northwest. Others believe they may have bypassed the glaciers by traveling down the West Coast in boats much earlier.

Nevertheless, living for so long in frozen conditions, they may have been startled as they continued to travel south and east and began to encounter warmer temperatures and the vast forests and fields of America's heartland.

Archaeologists are detectives, piecing together clues about ancient people from the things they left behind. Occasionally, they find tools, artwork, trash or the remains of the buildings of the earliest residents of the Northeast. However, these artifacts have often been scattered, broken or changed through the centuries, making it difficult to determine what the earliest people in the region were like or how they lived.

In the 1920s, stone arrowheads were found near Clovis,

Possible route of early humans into North America ➤

Asia · North Pole · Beringia land bridge · Alaska · Ice sheet · Atlantic Ocean · North America · Pacific Ocean

Events globally and locally

World events

	Dog domesticated in Middle East; brick houses built in Middle East	Wheat cultivated in Canaan (Israel)	Oldest city, Jericho, established	Cattle domesticated in Turkey; corn, beans and squash cultivated in Mexico	Cloth woven in Turkey

12,000 B.C.	11,000 B.C.	10,000 B.C.	9000 B.C.	8000 B.C.	7000 B.C.	6000 B.C.

Northeast events

Glaciers have retreated from the state and New England · The last mammoths and mastodons are dying off in the Northeast · Small family groups travel around the region to hunt, fish and gather fruits and nuts. · With the warmer climate, most modern species of native plants and animals now occupy the region

World events

Sail-propelled boats in Egypt	Wheeled vehicles in Sumer (Iraq)	Written language invented in Sumer	Alphabet used by Phoenicians	First known coins minted in Lydia (Turkey)	Writing paper first used in China	Gun or cannon first used in China

5000 B.C.	4000 B.C.	3000 B.C.	2000 B.C.	1000 B.C.	0	A.D. 1000

Northeast events

The Northeast's population peaks prior to widespread farming; perhaps several hundred thousand people · Copper introduced into region from Midwest · Clay pottery appears in region · Farming has become widespread; maize (corn) is a primary crop · First Europeans arrive

First humans in New Jersey

From the things that the earliest residents of New Jersey and surrounding states left behind, archaeologists have been able to determine some things about their lives in the region.

From the stone tools and rock formations of campsites, as well as the charcoal remains of campfires that are sometimes found, they are able to guess what animals those who lived in the camps were hunting, what their living quarters were like and whether they lived in large or small communities. They are able to estimate how old the campsite is within a few hundred years by using a technique called radiocarbon dating to estimate the age of the charcoal.

Some of the earliest and most abundant evidence of human beings in New Jersey comes from a site in Warren County, by the Musconetcong River, called the Plenge site, that may be 11,000 to 13,000 years old. More than a thousand artifacts, primarily projectile points, knives and scrapers as well as the rock flakes knocked off them during their creation, have been found there.

The Plenge site may have been used as a base camp that early hunters in the region returned to for hundreds of years as they moved between the Delaware River and the hunting grounds of northern New Jersey and New York state.

New Mexico, that date back perhaps 13,000 years. For many years, the Clovis date was accepted as the earliest date for humans in North America. However, evidence was discovered in the 1970s for a human presence in Pennsylvania that may be earlier than the Clovis dates.

The Meadowcroft Rockshelter is a shallow cave overlooking a creek in southwestern Pennsylvania. Radiocarbon dating, which is a method for measuring the age of carbon in things like charcoal and other once-living material, found that the site may have been used by humans 16,000 years ago and possibly as early as 19,000 years ago. However, not all archaeologists accept these earlier dates, believing the radiocarbon readings may be flawed.

Adding to the controversy is that sites that also have pre-Clovis dates have been found in other locations, including Virginia, Oregon, South Carolina and Texas as well as South America. So the question of when humans first reached the Americas is not settled.

Nevertheless, the first arrivals in North America, whom we now call "paleoindians," which means the oldest Indians, probably had lives some people today would envy. After all, many may have had a wealth of food, land to live on and leisure time.

Were they savages? Not at all, say anthropologists. They were just as intelligent and inventive as people today. Human beings have probably been thinking at our modern level of complexity for the past 50,000 years. That means there was just as much genius among these early people as there is among modern humans. There was also just as much greed, charity, cruelty and compassion then as now.

It's true that life for humans has changed dramatically over the centuries as inventions and discoveries have accumulated. But humans' basic emotional and intellectual makeup has changed

very little. If these early human cultures did not advance much beyond the use of simple tools, it's because there was little need for them to advance. By many standards, they were "rich" people. Their needs could be easily met. Indeed, they may have enjoyed life as much as many people today.

Paleoindians were a people frequently on the move, following the migration paths of the herd animals, such as caribou, or the waterfowl, such as ducks and geese, that they hunted. They also fished and trapped small game animals, such as beavers and rabbits, and they gathered and ate fruits, berries, nuts and some plants. In fact, plant matter may have made up much of their diet.

They probably carried their limited belongings on sleds or toboggans drawn by domesticated dogs or pulled by members of the group. Their tools included hammers, chisels, axes and awls (hole makers) made from rock, as well as other implements, such as sewing needles, made from bones or the ivory of mammoth tusks.

The sewing needle dates back at least 40,000 years. So the first Americans probably wore tailored clothes of furs and skins. And they probably lived in tents made of skins that had been loosely sewn together.

They would camp, possibly for weeks or months at a time, near where animals were known to seek food or water, for instance by a river, near a forest opening or around ponds or marshes. They would eventually move on, but if the hunting, fishing and berry picking were good enough, they might return to the same spot the next season.

The earliest residents of the Northeast probably had rich spiritual and social lives. Studies of modern-day hunting and gathering societies, such as those discovered in tropical rain forests, show they can be masters of conversation. Without tele-

Fishing line

Hooks were made of bone, and lines were weighted with a rock vision and books, talk is their main source of entertainment and information.

They also relied on speech to pass along the knowledge accumulated over thousands of years – effective herbal cures, tips for hunting game, and designs of tents or layouts of camps.

It is likely they passed their leisure time doing craftwork, playing with wooden toys or games, singing and dancing, and just absorbing the beautiful scenery.

As the number of people grew in a region, it is also likely that many families came together at certain times of the year for festivals where goods were traded, stories swapped and marriages arranged.

Certainly, medicine was not as advanced as it is today. But the simplicity of that era offered its own protection. The level of stress for many paleoindians was probably very low. With so much food and land, war was not yet common, although personal arguments and hostilities have always existed.

While more babies died in infancy than die today, those who survived childhood could often live into their forties or fifties. Native Americans did not suffer many of the

Ax
About 7 in. long; made perhaps 7,000 years ago.

medical problems that are now widespread, such as obesity, diabetes and high blood pressure, which often result from inactive lives and diets high in fat.

Indeed, when the first Europeans arrived in America, they were struck by the great health Native Americans seemed to enjoy.

What was life like for the Native Americans of the Northeast? For the centuries before Europeans settled widely in the region, life was simple in many respects and it was cyclical. It had the seasons as its clock.

Many Native American families would live by the seashore or a riverbank in summer, to fish andto gather food in nearby fields and forests. In winter, those by the coast might move to protected inland areas to hunt squirrels, beavers, deer, moose or bears and to live off stored supplies of vegetables, nuts and berries.

Farming became common in the Northeast about 1,000 years ago. Crops included maize (corn), beans, squash, pumpkins, cucumbers and tobacco. Villages often sat beside the agricultural fields. And a protective fence might be built around the edge of the village so that it could be a winter home or a fort.

To create open spaces for farming and for foot paths, Native Americans of the Northeast might periodically burn over the land, destroying the underbrush and many of the trees. The practice would also create more open land for hunting, and it would kill off insect pests near villages.

Crafting points for tools and weapons

Native Americans hunted game animals with spears and arrows and cleaned them with knives. The points on these tools and weapons were often made from rock called chert or flint. When chert was tapped with a sharp rock or other hard tool, flat flakes would come loose, allowing the rock to be fashioned into the desired shape.

Paleoindians would chisel grooves, called flutes, into the sides of the points so that once the point was finished, it might be tightly inserted into a notch in a stick. It was then tied into place with animal tendons, leather strips or other stringy material.

Points were sometimes made from other types of rock, including obsidian and quartzite.

Spear point
Made 5,000 to 6,000 years ago

Arrowhead
Made 500 to 2,000 years ago

Knife point
Made 5,000 to 7,000 years ago

The Lenape people of New Jersey

The Lenape, who were also called the Delaware people by Europeans, occupied the Delaware River basin. Their territory included all of New Jersey. The Lenape were divided into three major clans named after the wolf, the turtle and the turkey. Then there were several groups or tribes within each clan.

Unlike many other Native American groups, the Lenape were organized around the mother's family, and children traced their lineage through her.

If you were a Lenape, you might live in a village of 200 to 300 people, but most lived in smaller groups of 20 to 25 people.

Major tribes of the Northeast

Abenaki
Wenro
Iroquois Confederacy
Mahican
Pocumtuck
Erie
Susquehannock
Wappinger
LENAPE

The groups or tribes within the Lenape

Tappan
Hackensack
Raritan
Navesink
Sankhikan
Atsayonck
Remkoke
Armewarmex
Mantaes
Naraticonck
Little Siconese
Sewapois

Throughout the Northeast, Native American women were responsible for raising children, preparing meals and tending the crops and the home. Men were hunters, warriors and craftsmen, making the tools, utensils and weapons needed for survival.

Native American children, especially boys, were encouraged at a young age to be bold and self-reliant. To prove he had reached manhood, a young male might be led blindfolded into the woods in winter, armed with a bow and arrow, a knife and a hatchet, and be expected to survive on his own until spring.

The most common clothing for both men and women in warm weather was the breech clout, a belt and cloth that performed the same function as a pair of shorts does today. In colder weather, sewn layers of animal skins might be worn, often of raccoon or fox, with the fur side of the skin against the body.

Wigwams or wetus

Bark or woven mats were laid over frames made of branches. A hole in the roof allowed smoke from fires to escape.

When the first Europeans arrived in the region in the early 1600s, there may have been several hundred thousand Native Americans living in the Northeast.

However, diseases contracted from the earliest European trappers and traders – smallpox, measles, influenza, typhoid fever and tuberculosis – killed many Native Americans. They had no history of these new illnesses and little or no immunity to them.

The first epidemic of the European illnesses, believed to include smallpox, probably began in the early 1600s. By 1700, up to 90 percent of the Native Americans in some areas of the Northeast had died from the diseases.

Because of disease and wars with Europeans, by 1800 the Native American way of life, which had defined how humans lived in the region for nearly 100 centuries, had disappeared from much of the Northeast.

Some of the world's most magnificent mountains were once found in the Northeast. But that was hundreds of millions of years ago. All those years of rain and wind, and the freeze and thaw of water in their crevices, have steadily eroded these peaks. Today, mountains in the Northeast are minor when compared with mountains in other parts of the world.

There are 39 states with mountain peaks that rise higher above sea level than the tallest in New Jersey, High Point in the northwest highlands on the edge of the Appalachian Mountains. And at 1,803 feet above sea level, High Point is less than a 16th the height of the world's tallest mountain, Mount Everest. And it is less than on 11th the height of the tallest mountain in the United State, Denali in Alaska.

The high peaks of New Jersey are concentrated in the northwest in the highlands region. However, High Point is not actually a mountain. It is the highest point on the long ridge of Kittatinny Mountain that runs more than 30 miles along the New Jersey-Pennsylvania border.

Much of the central and southern part of the state is a coastal plain with elevations generally less than 200 feet.

Perhaps 460 million years ago, the collisions of continents drifting over the Earth's surface caused massive mountains to rise up on the land that is now New Jersey, peaks as high as the Rocky Mountains today. But in the overall time scheme of Earth, mountains can disappear in a flash. With an erosion rate of just a millimeter a year (.04 inches), even a very tall mountain can be reduced to almost nothing over a few million years.

Generally, the taller the mountain is, the higher the erosion rate. For one thing, the climate at a higher altitude is usually harsher. But the key is not the elevation; it is the slope. And higher mountain peaks usually have steeper slopes. Water loaded with sediments will run down a steep slope faster, wearing away the rock beneath it at a faster rate. Erosion is by no means a steady process, though. A landslide may remove a huge chunk of a mountain in a day, lowering a peak by dozens of feet. But over a million years, even with the occasional landslide, the erosion rate may average only a fraction of an inch each year.

Many believe that Mount Everest, the highest peak in the world at 29,029 feet above sea level, has had a rate of erosion over the last million or so years of about a centimeter (.4 inches) a year. Interestingly, the rate at which the peak is falling from erosion may be about the rate at which it is still rising, leaving the overall height of Everest stable.

The erosion rate for the Kittatinny Ridge and High Point is probably similar to that of other older mountain peaks in the Appalachians. One study in the Great Smoky Mountains estimated the rate there to be about .03 millimeters per year. That translates to erosion over a million years of about 100 feet.

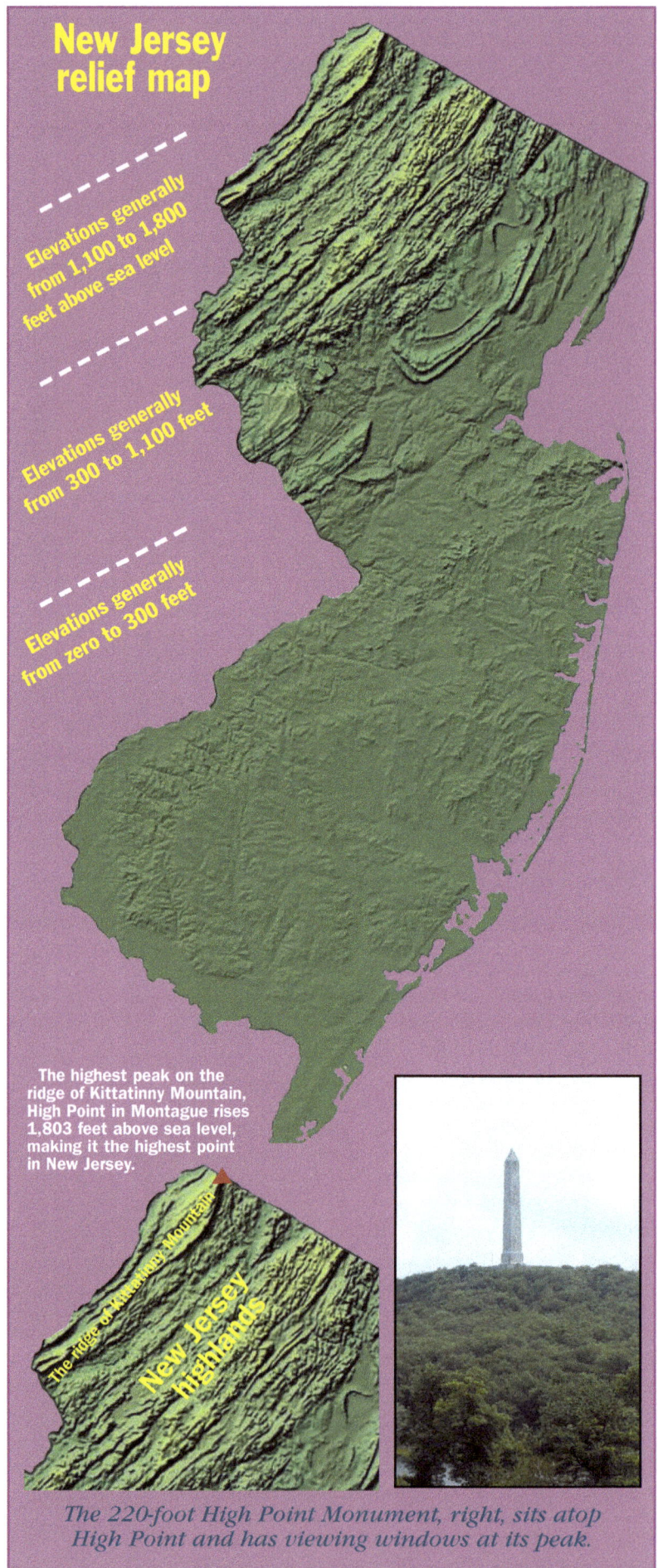

New Jersey relief map

Elevations generally from 1,100 to 1,800 feet above sea level

Elevations generally from 300 to 1,100 feet

Elevations generally from zero to 300 feet

The highest peak on the ridge of Kittatinny Mountain, High Point in Montague rises 1,803 feet above sea level, making it the highest point in New Jersey.

The ridge of Kittatinny Mountain

New Jersey highlands

The 220-foot High Point Monument, right, sits atop High Point and has viewing windows at its peak.

High peaks of New Jersey by county

(County – name of peak – feet above sea level)

1 Sussex – High Point – 1,803
2 Passaic – Bearfort Mt. – 1,480
3 Bergen – Bald Mtn. – 1,164
4 Hudson – Hudson County High Point – 260
5 Essex – Second Wachung Mt. – 660
6 Morris – Morris County High Point – 1,395
7 Warren – Kittatinny Mt. – 1,600
8 Hunterdon – Smith Benchmark or Camp Beisler South – 1,060
9 Somerset – Mine Mt. – 860
10 Union – High Point – 560
11 Middlesex – Sand Hills – 300
12 Mercer – Baldpate Mt. – 480
13 Monmouth – Crawford Hill – 380
14 Ocean – Ocean County High Point – 230
15 Burlington – Arneys Mount – 240
16 Camden – Camden County High Point – 219
17 Gloucester – Gloucester County High Point – 180
18 Atlantic – Atlantic County High Point – 150
19 Salem – Salem Cnty. High Point – 160
20 Cumberland – Cumberland County High Point – 140
21 Cape May – Cape May High Point – 60

The Appalachian National Scenic Trail

Usually called just the Appalachian Trail, it extends from Springer Mountain in Georgia to Mount Katahdin in Maine, traveling about 2,200 miles through 14 states, including New Jersey. The trail is maintained by various trail clubs and private landowners along the way, and it is managed by the National Park Service and the Appalachian Trail Conservancy.

The highest point in each U.S. state

(Height above sea level in feet)

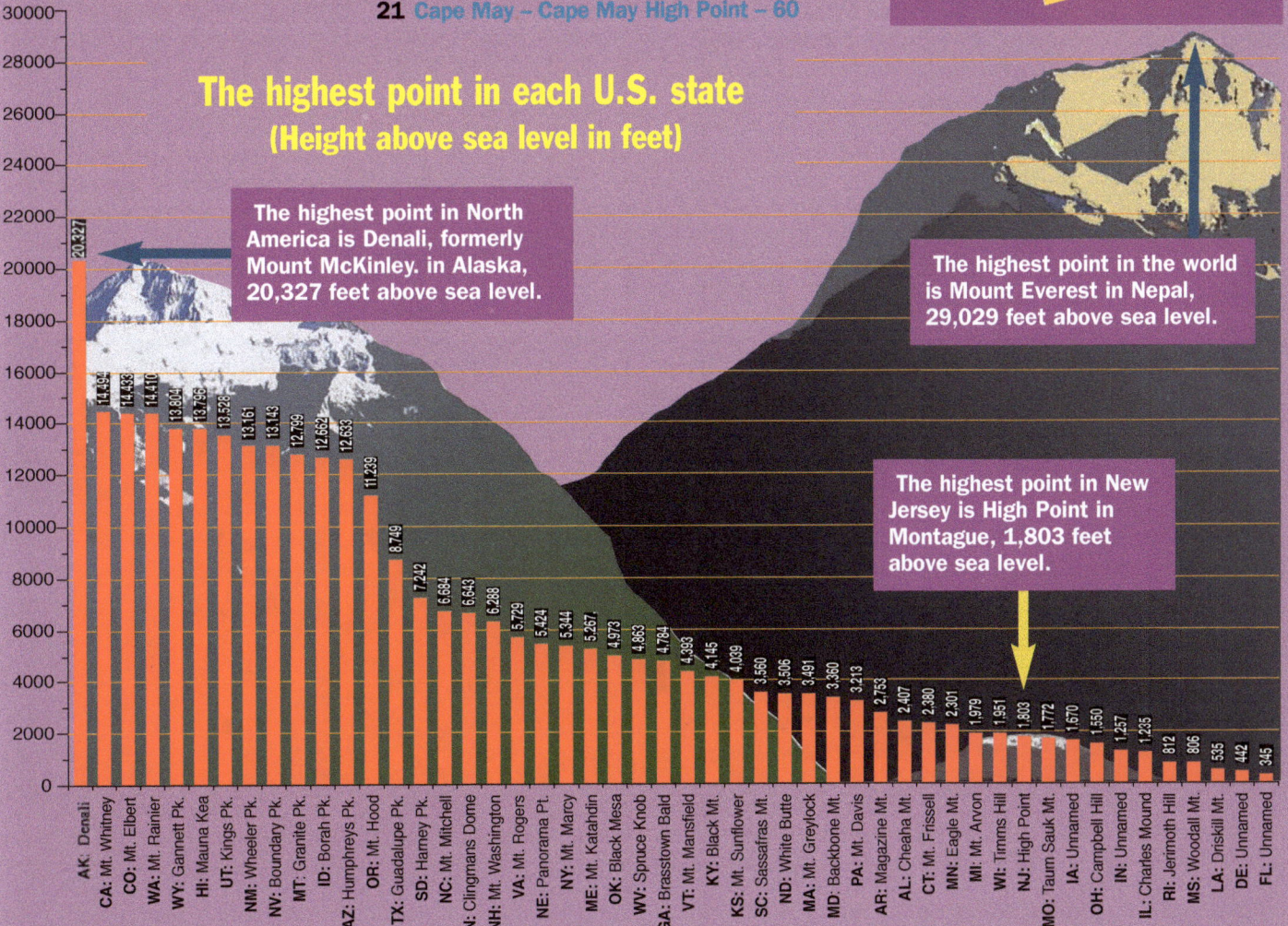

The highest point in North America is Denali, formerly Mount McKinley. in Alaska, 20,327 feet above sea level.

The highest point in the world is Mount Everest in Nepal, 29,029 feet above sea level.

The highest point in New Jersey is High Point in Montague, 1,803 feet above sea level.

State: Peak	Feet
AK: Denali	20,327
CA: Mt. Whitney	14,494
CO: Mt. Elbert	14,433
WA: Mt. Rainier	14,410
WY: Gannett Pk.	13,804
HI: Mauna Kea	13,796
UT: Kings Pk.	13,528
NM: Wheeler Pk.	13,161
NV: Boundary Pk.	13,143
MT: Granite Pk.	12,799
ID: Borah Pk.	12,662
AZ: Humphreys Pk.	12,633
OR: Mt. Hood	11,239
TX: Guadalupe Pk.	8,749
SD: Harney Pk.	7,242
NC: Mt. Mitchell	6,684
TN: Clingmans Dome	6,643
NH: Mt. Washington	6,288
VA: Mt. Rogers	5,729
NE: Panorama Pt.	5,424
NY: Mt. Marcy	5,344
ME: Mt. Katahdin	5,267
OK: Black Mesa	4,973
WV: Spruce Knob	4,863
GA: Brasstown Bald	4,784
VT: Mt. Mansfield	4,393
KY: Black Mt.	4,145
KS: Mt. Sunflower	4,039
SC: Sassafras Mt.	3,560
ND: White Butte	3,506
MA: Mt. Greylock	3,491
MD: Backbone Mt.	3,360
PA: Mt. Davis	3,213
AR: Magazine Mt.	2,753
AL: Cheaha Mt.	2,407
CT: Mt. Frissell	2,380
MN: Eagle Mt.	2,301
MI: Mt. Arvon	1,979
WI: Timms Hill	1,951
NJ: High Point	1,803
MO: Taum Sauk Mt.	1,772
IA: Unnamed	1,670
OH: Campbell Hill	1,550
IN: Unnamed	1,257
IL: Charles Mound	1,235
RI: Jerimoth Hill	812
MS: Woodall Mt.	806
LA: Driskill Mt.	535
DE: Unnamed	442
FL: Unnamed	345

You never have to travel far in New Jersey to find water. With more than 18,000 miles of rivers and streams as well as nearly 50,000 acres of lakes, ponds and reservoirs, 950,000 acres of wetlands, 260 square miles of estuaries, not to mention the Atlantic Ocean on its eastern coast, New Jersey has water, water everywhere – and quite a lot to drink.

Most people think of the Pacific Northwest as America's rain capital. In fact, Seattle gets less rainfall each year (an average of 38.8 inches) than Newark (46.2 inches).

The presence of so much water gives the state a great diversity of wildlife. There is a long list of plants and animals that live only in water, and another long list of wildlife that live alongside water.

The land surface of New Jersey slopes generally from the northwest highlands to the south and east. Water from most of the state's rivers generally follows these same slopes and eventually ends up in the Atlantic Ocean or the bays, such as Delaware Bay, that adjoin the Atlantic. Some streams and rivers in the western part of the state also flow west into the Delaware River.

There are exceptions, though. The Wallkill River flows north into the Hudson River, even though the Hudson River, to the east, and the Delaware River, to the west, flow south.

A half century ago, several of the state's major rivers were polluted eyesores because of the sewage, chemicals and trash that were being dumped into them. But citizen and government action to clean up these waterways, including the construction of sewage treatment plants, has turned many of them into clean rivers. However, pollution in some waterways, especially those in areas where industries lined their banks, such as the lower section of the Passacic River, was so overwhelming that efforts to clean them up have not yet succeeded.

The drinking water of New Jersey comes primarily from reservoirs, rivers and underground aquifers. Aquifers are often found in underground layers of sand and gravel or in rock, such as limestone, that has holes, crevices or caves in it. Beneath the aquifer is solid rock through which the water cannot pass, so it acts like a bowl holding the water.

Nearly a trillion gallons of fresh water are used each year in the state. Most of it, about 59 percent, is drawn from rivers other than the Delaware River, which accounts for 7 percent of the withdrawals. About 23 percent of the fresh water comes from wells that tap aquifers. Reservoirs contribute about 11 percent.

Lake Wawayanda in Wawayanda State Park in Hewitt

Lake or pond?

The usual definition of a pond is that it is shallow enough for aquatic plants to grow anywhere in it. But a lake can be so deep and dark in places that plants only grow in the shallow areas.

Wetlands

Between dry land and the deep water of lakes, rivers or the ocean, you will often see wetlands, areas where land and water mix, such as swamps, marshes, bogs, wet meadows and riverbank forests that may flood after heavy rains.

Wetlands were once considered places of no value in much of America, and in the last two centuries more than half the acreage of wetlands in the lower 48 states has been filled, drained or otherwise lost.

But wetlands do have great value, people have learned. They filter out pollution before it reaches larger bodies of water, and they are home to many kinds of plants and animals, from cattails to muskrats, that are seen almost nowhere else. That's why wetlands are now protected by law.

Since 1780 in New Jersey, nearly 39 percent of the state's wetlands has disappeared. The state now has about 916,000 acres of freshwater and saltwater wetlands, with most of them found in the coastal plain.

Lily pads

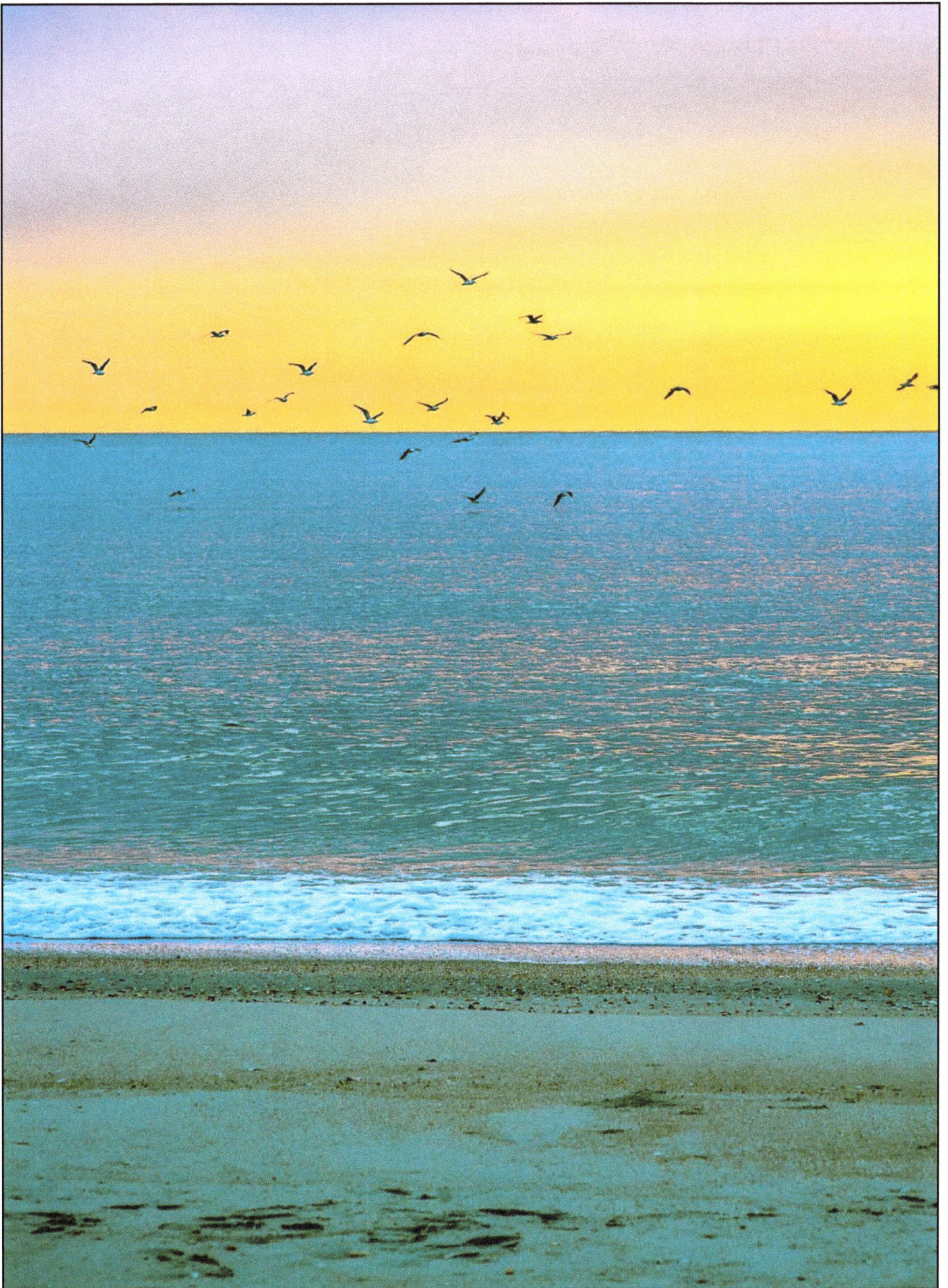
Sunrise on a beach on Sandy Hook in Middletown Township on the Jersey Shore

Delaware River

Length: 330 miles
Source: Uplands of Schoharie County, N.Y.
Mouth: Delaware Bay in Delaware and New Jersey

Hudson River

Length: 315 miles
Source: Lake Tear of Clouds on Mount Marcy in Essex County, N.Y.
Mouth: Atlantic Ocean

Passaic River

Length: 80 miles
Source: A pond in Mendham, N.J.
Mouth: Newark Bay in Newark

Great Egg Harbor River

Length: 55 miles
Source: Near Berlin, N.J.
Mouth: Great Egg Harbor

Hackensack River

Length: 54 miles
Source: West Haverstraw, N.Y.
Mouth: Newark Bay

Toms River

Length: 42 miles
Source: The pine barrens in Ocean County
Mouth: Barnegat Bay

Raritan River

Length: 30 miles
Source: The joining of the south and north branches of the Raritan River in Bridgewater
Mouth: Raritan Bay south of Perth Amboy, N.J.

Delaware R.
Paulins Kill
Wallkill R.
Wanaque Res.
Lake Hopatcong
Hackensack R.
Musconetcong R.
Passaic R.
Passaic R.
Hudson R.
Jersey City
Newark
Round Valley Res.
Arthur Kill
Raritan R.
Millstone R.
Sandy Hook Bay
Delaware R.
Trenton
Rancocas Cr.
Toms R.
Camden
Delaware R.
Barnegat Bay
Mannington Meadows
Mullica R.
Wading R.
Great Egg Harbor R.
Great Bay
Cohansey R.
Maurice R.
Great Egg Harbor
Atlantic Ocean
Delaware Bay

A tale of two rivers

The Passaic River – Bucolic and peaceful, a natural haven for birds and other wildlife, surrounded by meadows, wetlands and floodplain forests; once immortalized by famed American author Washington Irving as a river that flows "gentle and clear" in a "wild, tranquil vale, fringed with forests of green ... where nature had fashion'd a soft, sylvan scene."

The Passaic River – A polluted eyesore, its waters fouled and blackened by industrial wastes, its shores littered with garbage; once called by famed American poet and New Jersey resident William Carlos Williams, "The vilest swill hole in Christendom."

Which is it?

Ironically, both.

The stretch of the 80-mile river above Paterson remains a largely protected, pristine waterway that in many stretches bears a resemblance to the river that the Lenape once depended on for sustenance, for water, fish and shellfish. However, the stretch from Paterson to where the river empties into Newark Bay shows the consequence of the intense industrialization of that portion of New Jersey after 1850.

Unfortunately, environmental officials are finding it difficult to turn back the clock on the polluted lower portion of the Passaic, as the poisons, including dioxin, that were dumped in the river by the businesses that settled on its banks are proving persistent.

Indeed, in the battle to clean up the Passaic, which has already seen tens of millions of dollars spent for filtering, dredging and other cleansing techniques, the pollution seems to be winning. The lower stretch is still considered one of the most polluted river sections in the nation and it is forbidden to eat the fish and shellfish caught in it.

In March, 2016, the U.S. Environmental Protection Agency announced a $1.4 billion plan to clean up the most polluted portion of the Passaic, the lower eight miles. The EPA wants the project, which will last more than 11 years, to be paid for by the nearly 100 companies that were responsible for polluting the river.

The plan calls for the river to be dredged, the sediment disposed of elsewhere, and for a two-foot thick cap made of sand and stone, to be placed over the riverbed through its entire eight-mile length.

Great Falls on the Passaic River in Paterson

Annual snowfall
(in inches)

- 55-62
- 43-55
- 33-43
- 27-33
- 21-27
- 15-21

Fall foliage
(When to see peak autumn colors)

Annual precipitation
(in inches)

- Less than 42
- 42-44
- 44-46
- 46-48
- 48-50
- 50-52
- 52-54
- More than 54

Fall foliage legend:
- Oct. 1 to Oct. 12
- Oct. 3 to Oct. 15
- Oct. 5 to Oct. 18
- Oct. 12 to Oct. 25
- Oct. 15 to Oct. 29
- Oct. 23 to Nov. 5

Sunrise and sunset in New Jersey

Jan. Mar. May July Sept. Nov. Jan.

DAYLIGHT-SAVING TIME

Time of sunset

Daylight-saving time – From the second Sunday in March to the first Sunday in November, the times for sunrise and sunset are set one hour later.

The fewest hours of daylight occur Dec. 21 in Trenton – 9 hrs., 18 min.

The most hours of daylight occur June 20 in Trenton – 15 hrs., 2 min.

Time of sunrise

DAYLIGHT-SAVING TIME

Feb. Apr. June Aug. Oct. Dec.

8 p.m., 6 p.m., 4 p.m., 2 p.m., Noon, 10 a.m., 8 a.m., 6 a.m., 4 a.m.

Typical sunrise and sunset time for Trenton by month

Jan. 1: 7:21 a.m., 4:43 p.m.
Feb. 1: 7:08 a.m., 5:17 p.m.
March 1: 6:32 a.m., 5:51 p.m.
April 1: 6:42 a.m., 7:24 p.m.
May 1: 5:58 a.m., 7:55 p.m.
June 1: 5:31 a.m., 8:23 p.m.
July 1: 5:33 a.m., 8:32 p.m.
Aug. 1: 5:57 a.m., 8:13 p.m.
Sept. 1: 6:27 a.m., 7:30 p.m.
Oct. 1: 6:56 a.m., 6:40 p.m.
Nov. 1: 7:29 a.m., 5:56 p.m.
Dec. 1: 7:03 a.m., 4:34 p.m.

Newark	Jan.	Feb.	Mar.	Apr.	May	June	July	Aug.	Sep.	Oct.	Nov.	Dec.	Total or annual avg.
Snowfall (inches)	8.9	9.5	4.4	.9	0	0	0	0	0	0	.4	5.4	29.5
Precipitation (inches)	3.53	2.88	4.18	4.20	4.09	4.02	4.76	3.70	3.82	3.60	3.65	3.80	46.24
Avg. daily max. temp.	38.8	42.3	50.7	62.0	72.1	81.5	86.0	84.0	76.7	65.3	54.6	43.5	63.1
Avg. daily min. temp.	24.5	26.9	33.6	43.7	53.3	63.3	68.7	67.5	59.7	48.0	39.0	29.6	46.5
Precipitation days (avg.)*	10.4	9.8	11.0	11.5	11.3	11.0	10.1	9.7	8.6	8.7	9.5	10.6	122.1
Snow days (avg.)**	5.0	3.7	2.4	.4	0	0	0	0	0	0	.4	2.9	14.7

*Precipitation greater or equal to .01 inches   **Snowfall greater or equal to .1 inches

Atlantic City	Jan.	Feb.	Mar.	Apr.	May	June	July	Aug.	Sep.	Oct.	Nov.	Dec.	Total or annual avg.
Snowfall (inches)	4.5	6.7	1.1	.3	0	0	0	0	0	0	.2	3.7	16.5
Precipitation (inches)	3.08	2.87	4.02	3.39	3.22	2.68	3.31	3.92	3.08	3.47	3.35	3.62	40.01
Avg. daily max. temp.	41.8	43.5	49.6	57.6	66.6	75.7	81.3	80.2	74.8	65.0	55.8	46.3	61.6
Avg. daily min. temp.	29.2	30.9	36.9	45.5	54.5	64.3	70.0	69.7	63.5	52.5	42.9	33.5	49.5
Precipitation days (avg.)*	9.3	9.0	10.5	10.9	10.4	8.7	8.4	8.0	7.7	7.6	8.9	10.4	109.8
Snow days (avg.)**	2.9	2.8	.9	.3	0	0	0	0	0	0	.1	1.7	8.7

Hurricane Sandy

The most costly storm in New Jersey's recorded history and the second costliest storm in U.S. history, Hurricane Sandy came ashore just northeast of Atlantic City early on Oct. 29, 2012.

By the time the eye made landfall in the state, the hurricane had diminished in power to a post-tropical cyclone. So it was not the wind, which still reached speeds of 80 miles per hour, so much as the surge of water created by the storm that devastated coastal New Jersey.

And indeed, it was devastating. The famed Jersey Shore lost 30 to 40 feet of beachfront in most sections due to the storm's huge waves and fierce erosive power. In Mantoloking on the barrier islands, nearly two dozen homes were washed off their foundations and destroyed. A 50-foot section of the Atlantic City boardwalk was washed away and much of the Seaside Heights boardwalk, including the roller coaster, collapsed into the Atlantic because of the intense waves.

The massive amount of rain during the storm caused great flooding inland as well. Nearly a foot of rain fell in some communities. Half the city of Hoboken ended up underwater, leading to evacuations of two fire stations and the hospital. Half the residents of Jersey City lost power and a large section of the downtown, including City Hall and the Medical Center, flooded and had to be evacuated.

Statewide, more than 2.6 million customers lost power during Sandy and nearly 90 percent of schools had to be closed.

Five months later, some 39,000 New Jersey families were still unable to return to their homes because of the damage Sandy had wrought.

In the end, nearly $30 billion in damages was sustained in the state and 37 people lost their lives. A federal study estimated that some 72,000 homes and business in New Jersey were damaged or destroyed by Hurricane Sandy.

Only Hurricane Katrina in 2005 caused most costly damage in this country.

The damage caused by Hurricane Sandy on the pier at Seaside Heights, N.J.

NEW JERSEY NATURE CALENDAR

January

1	2	3	4	5	6	7
Brown trout eggs, laid in gravel-bottomed streams in fall, are slowly developing.			Red-spotted newts are active under the ice all winter.		Bullfrogs are settled in the mud at the bottom of ponds, waiting for the spring thaw.	

8	9	10	11	12	13	14
Trees are in a semi-dormant state, living off stored nutrients.		Many white-tailed deer lose their antlers in coming weeks and regrow them in the spring.			Watch for red-tailed hawks perched in roadside trees, searching for prey below.	

15	16	17	18	19	20	21
The coldest temperatures, strongest winds and heaviest snowfalls of the year may occur about now.			Eagles from the north will migrate into New Jersey in winter to fish the open waters of larger lakes, rivers and reservoirs.			

22	23	24	25	26	27	28
Female red foxes are establishing their dens, preparing to bear young later in the spring.			Raccoons, beavers and gray squirrels are entering their breeding seasons.			Black bear cubs are being born in winter dens.

29	30	31				
On warm days this time of year, bluebottle flies may emerge in attics and in sunny unused rooms.						

February

1	2	3	4	5	6	7
Coyotes are breeding.	Great horned owls are beginning to nest, one of the first birds to do so each year.			On the south side of trees, look for snow fleas, which may resemble small black specks.		

8	9	10	11	12	13	14
Beneath the ice on frozen lakes and ponds, bluegills and sunfish are nearly dormant, but yellow perch, bass and trout are still active.				Skunks are venturing out to breed. Their scent is a sign spring is approaching.		

15	16	17	18	19	20	21
Ring-necked ducks begin migrating through the state as they fly north to nest in northern New York and Canada.				The first killdeer of the season may show up on plowed fields free of snow.		Maple sap begins to run about this time.

22	23	24	25	26	27	28
Flocks of red-winged blackbirds and common grackles are returning from the south.			Cardinals and chickadees are beginning to sing their spring songs.			Turkey vultures are returning to the region.

29						
Leap day occurs every fourth year.						

NEW JERSEY NATURE CALENDAR

March

1	2	3	4	5	6	7
Mourning cloak butterflies, which spend the winter in tree cavities and other hidden places, may emerge on especially warm days.				Peregrine falcons are returning to their nests in cities and elsewhere in New Jersey.		

8	9	10	11	12	13	14
Red-tailed hawks are building their nests.		Barred owls are in their mating season.		Black bears, snapping turtles, garter snakes and chipmunks are coming out of winter dormancy.		

15	16	17	18	19	20	21
Skunk cabbage may be emerging in wetlands.		The first robin may appear on lawns if the snow has disappeared.			The vernal equinox happens about the 21st, marking the start of spring.	

22	23	24	25	26	27	28
In most years, ice is disappearing from lakes and ponds about now.		If there is heavy rain, earthworms may emerge in lawns. Robins will be waiting.			The young of river otters, red foxes and gray squirrels are being born.	

29	30	31				
The call of wood frogs, which sounds like a duck quacking, can be heard around woodland ponds.						

April

1	2	3	4	5	6	7
On the first warm rainy night in mid-March to early April, several species of salamanders, as well as wood frogs, migrate to vernal pools to lay eggs.					Cabbage white butterflies are on the wing.	

8	9	10	11	12	13	14
Buds are appearing on many trees.		Male American goldfinches are molting as they lose their dull winter coloring.				Grass may be turning green.

15	16	17	18	19	20	21
Some woodland wildflowers bloom about now, before trees grow their leaves and cut off the sunlight.				Dandelions are appearing.		The last flurries of snow may be seen about now.

22	23	24	25	26	27	28
The last freezing temperatures of the spring may occur at night about now.			Common violets are appearing on lawns. Look for the occasional white violet in the mix.			Wild columbine is starting to bloom.

29	30					
Bobcats, raccoons and porcupines are having their young.						

NEW JERSEY NATURE CALENDAR

May

1	2	3	4	5	6	7
Ruby-throated hummingbirds are returning from the south.		Snakes and turtles spend the day basking in the sun to warm their bodies.			The leaves on most trees have fully opened. Sugar maples will leaf out before red maples.	

8	9	10	11	12	13	14
Warblers have been arriving from the south in recent weeks.		Many songbirds, including robins, cardinals and chickadees, are laying eggs.			The young of mallards and other ducks are hatching. Within a day they will take to water.	

15	16	17	18	19	20	21
Jack-in-the-pulpits are blooming.		Many butterflies are out, including eastern black swallowtails and little wood satyrs.			Downy woodpeckers are laying their eggs in tree cavities.	

22	23	24	25	26	27	28
Wild lupines are flowering in meadows.		Wood turtles are laying eggs in areas of sand or gravel.				Violets are disappearing from lawns and fields.

29	30	31				
Treefrogs are in their breeding season and are most likely to be seen this time of year.						

June

1	2	3	4	5	6	7
Monarch butterflies are returning to the region.			White-tailed deer are having their young.		June bugs are emerging, often swarming around porch lights.	

8	9	10	11	12	13	14
Painted and snapping turtles are climbing out of ponds to lay their eggs.				Fragrant water lilies are blooming in ponds and Queen Anne's lace is flowering along roadsides.		

15	16	17	18	19	20	21
Black-eyed Susans, oxeye daisies and other field wildflowers are coming into bloom.				Day lilies are blooming.	The summer solstice happens about the 21st, marking the start of summer.	

22	23	24	25	26	27	28
Snakes that lay eggs, such as milk snakes, are doing so about now. Other snakes, like garter snakes, have live young later in the season.					The flashing of fireflies can be seen at night above fields and meadows.	

29	30					
Bears are in the heart of their breeding season.						

NEW JERSEY NATURE CALENDAR

July

1	2	3	4	5	6	7
The young of many raptors, such as red-tailed hawks and great horned owls, are fully grown and out on their own by now.				The season's second generation of clouded sulphur and spring azure butterflies is emerging.		

8	9	10	11	12	13	14
Butter and eggs is in bloom along roadsides and in meadows.		Wild blueberries are ripening.		The greatest amount of sunshine and the least cloudiness during daylight hours occurs about this time of year.		

15	16	17	18	19	20	21
Katydids and crickets can be heard calling at night.		The whine of cicadas can be heard during the heat of the day.				Tadpoles are emerging from green frog eggs.

22	23	24	25	26	27	28
The flutelike trill of gray treefrogs can be heard on cloudy days.		Chipmunks may be having their second litter of young this year.			The delicate orange flowers of jewelweed, also called touch-me-not, are in bloom.	

29	30	31
The hottest days of summer may occur about now and into early August.		

August

1	2	3	4	5	6	7
Goldfinches are beginning to nest, among the latest of any of the songbirds to do so.			With the breeding season for frogs over, ponds have become quiet.		Garter snakes may be having their young.	

8	9	10	11	12	13	14
Grasshopper and yellow jacket populations are increasing.		Shooting stars from the annual Perseid meteor shower can be seen at night.			Great blue herons have abandoned their nests for the season.	

15	16	17	18	19	20	21
Many types of goldenrod are blooming in fields and along roadsides. Joe-Pye weed is blooming around wetlands.					On rainy days, red-spotted newts can be seen on dirt roads in rural areas.	

22	23	24	25	26	27	28
The season's third generation of cabbage white butterflies is emerging.			The final heat wave of the summer may occur about now.		Leopard frogs can sometimes be seen in back yards.	

29	30	31
Tree swallows have moved to coastal areas, preparing to migrate.		

NEW JERSEY NATURE CALENDAR

September

1	2	3	4	5	6	7

The eggs of wood, painted and snapping turtles are hatching.

Wild cherries and wild grapes are ripening.

Ladybugs may gather on light-colored house trim this month looking for places to enter homes to spend the winter.

8	9	10	11	12	13	14

Female ruby-throated hummingbirds and their young are migrating south. Males tend to leave one or two weeks earlier.

It's the peak of the migration south for songbirds and hawks.

15	16	17	18	19	20	21

Acorns and other nuts are ripening and dropping. Squirrels and bears are feeding heavily on them, fattening up for winter.

Monarch butterflies are migrating to their winter home in the mountains of central Mexico.

22	23	24	25	26	27	28

The autumnal equinox occurs about the 23rd, marking the start of fall.

Asters are blooming.

Green darner dragonflies are migrating south, one of the few dragonflies that does migrate. Most adults of other species die in the fall.

29	30					

Bats that migrate south for the winter are leaving the area.

October

1	2	3	4	5	6	7

Woodchucks are feeding on grass, putting on fat for hibernation.

Dark-eyed juncos are just arriving for the cold months. Slate gray above and white below, they often look for seeds on the ground beneath bird feeders.

8	9	10	11	12	13	14

Bullfrogs, snapping turtles and garter snakes are entering hibernation. The warmer the autumn, the later this will happen.

Fall foliage colors in much of the region are at their peak.

15	16	17	18	19	20	21

Listen for spring peepers calling in the woods on especially warm days.

White-tailed deer are in their mating seasons. It is the time of year you're most likely to see a buck as the males are traveling widely to find a mate.

22	23	24	25	26	27	28

The first flurries of snow for the season may be seen about now.

The baby spiders of some species are emerging from eggs. Others wait until spring.

Once a frost occurs, goldenrod starts to disappear from fields and roadsides.

29	30	31				

Humpback whales are migrating out of New Jersey coastal waters and will head to warm tropical waters for the winter.

NEW JERSEY NATURE CALENDAR

November

1	2	3	4	5	6	7
Chipmunks are storing acorns in their underground burrows, readying for winter.			Flocks of cedar waxwings may be migrating through the region.		Crows begin to gather in nightly roosts and will continue to do so until spring.	

8	9	10	11	12	13	14
Dandelions may still be blooming in protected areas.			The last faint call of meadow crickets can be heard on warm afternoons.		Woodchucks go into hibernation about now.	

15	16	17	18	19	20	21
Eastern cottontails are out foraging for twigs and buds as well as the seedlings of maples, birches and oaks.			Black bears are looking for a winter den. Their body temperature will remain too high for their sleep to be true hibernation.			

22	23	24	25	26	27	28
Beavers are cutting tender branches and storing them near their lodges as a food supply for winter.				Migrating Canada geese, flying in "V" formations, can be seen and heard overhead.		

29	30					
The coats of snowshoe hares, which are brown in summer, are turning white about now for winter protection.						

December

1	2	3	4	5	6	7
Wood frogs and spring peepers are burrowed in the dead leaves on the forest floor, some nearly frozen solid as they hibernate for the winter.					If the weather is normal, ponds may begin to freeze over about now.	

8	9	10	11	12	13	14
Muskrats are still active, feeding on submerged roots and lily stalks in ponds and lakes.				Shooting stars from the annual Geminid meteor shower can be seen on clear nights.		

15	16	17	18	19	20	21
Bobcats, foxes and coyotes are still active as are snowshoe hares and white-footed mice – their prey.				The winter solstice occurs about the 21st, marking the start of winter.		

22	23	24	25	26	27	28
Male hairy woodpeckers may try to attract females by drumming loudly on the sides of houses or on gutters.				Great horned owls can be heard hooting as they establish territories.		

29	30	31				
With so many birds gone for the winter, blue jays and crows are especially conspicuous.						

Peregrine falcon

The Natural History of New Jersey

Published by:
Hampshire House Publishing Co.
8 Nonotuck St.
Florence, Mass. 01062
www.hampshirehousepub.com

Printed in the USA
Copyright © 2017 by Stan Freeman and Mike Nasuti
ISBN: 97809893333-5-1

Some of the material in this book is based on articles by the authors that originally appeared in The Republican of Springfield, Mass.

The authors would like to thank the New Jersey state environmental and wildlife agencies for their help in   preparing this book or for the permission they gave us for material used in it.

If you find what you believe is an error, please notify us by email at hamphouse@comcast.net. The books are printed as they are ordered, which means we can upload a corrected digital file to the printer overnight and the new version will be in print the following day.

Facts and figures change, and every other year around Jan. 1, we may update the book, even adding new material.

Photography credits

All photos are by Stan Freeman unless otherwise noted. A photograph's position on a page is indicated as follows: T = top, C = center, B = bottom, R = right, L = left and A = all photos on page or in the indicated region of page.

Holly Schlacter Lowe – 12T, 12CL, 12C; Frandy Johnson – 30L; Illinois Department of Natural Resources – 27TR, 28BL, 28BR, 34B, 37TC; U.S. Centers for Disease Control – 43BR, 57CL, 57CR; U.S. Fish & Wildlife Service – 27 (gray wolf), 27 (red wolf), 33B, 38BC, 42TR, 47CL, 55B, 65, 66CR, 75T, 76BR, 78B, 79, 87, 115; U.S. Department of Agriculture – 61CR; Smithsonian – 92C; National Oceanic and Atmospheric Administration – 67TL, 67TR, 68TL, 68BR; Corel – 2T, 11TL, 13A, 14A, 15TR, 15B, 18T, 21CL (hawk), 23A, 24BL, 27 (western coyote), 29B, 30BR, 30CR, 31A, 36BL, 40BL, 40BR, 41CR, 66CL, 66CR, 68CL, 69TR, 70CL, 70CR; Shutterstock – 1T, 5, 18BR, 22, 25, 30TR, 32, 35C, 39, 43T, 47CL, 48T, 52TR, 54B, 55TL, 56TR, 57BR, 61TR, 61CL, 69B, 71, 80TC, 81T, 85R, 92TR, 94TR, 103, 105, front cover; New Jersey Army National Guard – 107; New Jersey Division of Parks and Forestry – 100BR, 102TR; Massachusetts Office of Travel and Tourism – 68BL, 68TR, 69TL, 72BR, 73, 75B, 99B
Front cover photo: Black bear

Coyote howling at the moon

This series highlights the natural history of individual states in the Northeast. We began with a basic book, essentially a collection of articles, and we are attempting to adapt it to each state in the series. So some material in this book, including text, illustrations and photographs, is repeated from book to book in the series.